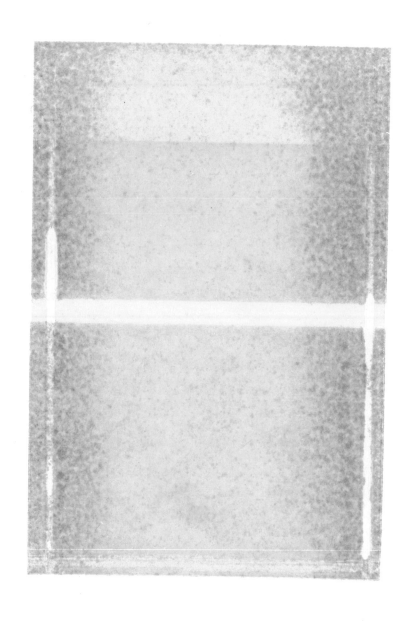

4-18-66

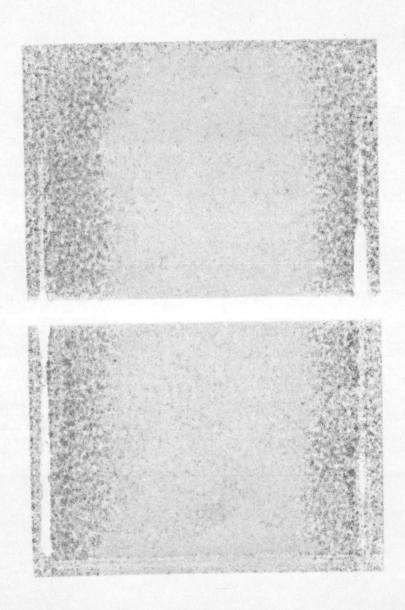

Adam Silver

1765-1795

Faber Monographs on Silver

GENERAL EDITOR: A. G. GRIMWADE F.S.A.

★

ADAM SILVER by Robert Rowe
HUGUENOT SILVER IN ENGLAND 1688–1727
by J. F. Hayward

(in preparation)

RESTORATION SILVER by C. C. Oman
REGENCY SILVER by Judith Banister
ELIZABETHAN SILVER by Gerald Taylor
SPOONS by Mrs. G. E. P. How
VICTORIAN SILVER by Mrs. Shirley Bury
ROCOCO SILVER by A. G. Grimwade

Cup and cover, gilt. Charles Wright, 1774.
Victoria and Albert Museum

ADAM SILVER

1765-1795

by

ROBERT ROWE

TAPLINGER PUBLISHING CO., INC.

New York

First American Edition published by
TAPLINGER PUBLISHING CO., INC., 1965

Library of Congress Catalogue Card Number : 65–20355

Made and Printed in Great Britain
© Faber and Faber Limited 1965

To
E.M.S.R.

1356842

Acknowledgements

In writing this book I have paid particular attention to contemporary records and when quoting from them have done as little editing as possible. By the middle of the eighteenth century documentation becomes vast and constitutes a veritable gold-mine of information there for the digging. Moreover the literary style of the day had such lucidity as well as charm that one can often learn as much from the way something is said as from the factual details given.

Very few of the letters in the important collection of Matthew Boulton papers at the Assay Office in Birmingham have been published and I have therefore seized the opportunity of improving the situation a little. I am indebted to Mr. Westwood, the Assay Master, for allowing me to publish the letters quoted from in Chapters 4, 5 and 7 all of which, with the exception of those written by Josiah Wedgwood, are in the Assay Office collection. I have not altered the original spelling as this is usually colourful and unambiguous. I am also grateful to Mr. Westwood for giving me ready access to the material under his care over the course of several years, for advice, and for reading the relevant parts of the book before going to press.

I would like to thank too Mr. Oman of the Victoria and Albert Museum for generous help and guidance on numerous occasions; Mr. Seaby of the Ulster Museum, Belfast, for lending me his photographs and notes on Matthew Boulton; Mr. Grimwade, editor of this series, for information about the Crespell brothers, Thomas Pitts and the firm of Parker and Wakelin; Mr. Ronald Wilson of the Sheffield Smelting Company for allowing me to peruse the archives of his firm; and Sir John Summerson for aid in identifying drawings in the Soane Museum.

Amongst those who have helped with photographs and in many other ways I would like particularly to thank Mrs. Buhler of the Museum of Fine Arts, Boston, Mass.; Mrs. Hunter of the Art

Acknowledgements

Reference Library, San Marino; Mr. Schubart of the City Art Gallery, Bristol; Mr. Singleton of the City Museum, Sheffield; Mr. Corbett of the British Museum; and Miss Norris of the Birmingham Reference Library.

Special thanks are due to Miss Elizabeth Murdoch for all her work in the preparation of this book, particularly in checking up complicated references in libraries at too great a distance from me to be readily accessible.

Finally I am indebted to the following private owners, public bodies and dealers who have allowed me to reproduce the illustrations. I gratefully acknowledge their kindness :

Sir William Brooksbank, Bt.,
Mrs. Hiatt-Baker,
George Howard, Esq.,
Mr. and Mrs. R. P. Kellett,
The Earl of Lonsdale,
Dr. C. G. Kay Sharp,
The Marquess of Zetland,
Messrs. John Bell of Aberdeen,
Messrs. Christie, Manson & Woods, Ltd.,
Messrs. Thomas Lumley, Ltd.,
Messrs. S. J. Phillips, Ltd.,
Messrs. Sotheby & Co.,
The Assay Office, Birmingham,
The Museum and Art Gallery, Birmingham,
The Reference Library, Birmingham,
The Museum of Fine Arts, Boston, Mass.,
The City Art Gallery, Bristol,
The Master and Fellows of Pembroke College, Cambridge,
The Master and Fellows of Trinity Hall, Cambridge,
The National Museum of Wales, Cardiff,
The Royal Scottish Museum, Edinburgh,
The Trustees and Members of the Leeds Art Collections Fund,
The Print Room and Art Library, Leeds,
Temple Newsam House, Leeds,
The City of Liverpool Museums,
The Walker Art Gallery, Liverpool,
The British Museum,
The Master and Wardens of the Drapers' Company, London,
Lloyd's of London,

Acknowledgements

The Royal Academy of Arts, London,
The Trustees of Sir John Soane's Museum, London,
The Victoria and Albert Museum,
The City of Manchester Art Galleries,
The Ashmolean Museum, Oxford,
The Sheffield City Museum,
Kungl Livrustkammeren, Stockholm.

Contents

Illustrations

Cup and cover, gilt. Charles Wright, 1774. Victoria and Albert Museum *frontispiece*

---

at the end of the book

1. Soup tureen, gilt, one of a pair. Daniel Smith and Robert Sharp, 1776. Messrs. Lumley
2. Wood and Dawkins: 'Palmyra' 1753, Plate XXIV. Print Room and Art Library, Leeds
3. d'Hancarville: William Hamilton's Collection, 1766–7, Vol. I Plate 74. British Museum
4A. Wood and Dawkins: 'Balbec' 1757, Plate XX. Print Room and Art Library, Leeds
4B. Wood and Dawkins: 'Balbec' 1757, Plate XXX. Print Room and Art Library, Leeds
5. Wood and Dawkins: 'Palmyra' 1753, Plate XIX. Print Room and Art Library, Leeds
6. Robert Adam: Drawing inscribed 'Vase for Thomas Dundass Esqʳ for a Prize'. Sir John Soane's Museum
7. Robert Adam: Drawing inscribed 'Vase for Thomas Dundas Esqʳ for a Prize'. Sir John Soane's Museum
8. The Richmond Race Cup, gilt. Daniel Smith and Robert Sharp, 1770. Marquess of Zetland
9. The Richmond Race Cup (detail)
10. Candlestick, one of a pair. John Carter, 1767. Temple Newsam House, Leeds
11A. Adam Drawing, inscribed 'Design of a Candlestick'. Sir John Soane's Museum
11B. Two Adam Drawings, both inscribed 'Plan of bottom of Candlestick'. Sir John Soane's Museum
12. Candelabrum, one of a set of four. John Carter, 1774. Lloyd's of London

[15]

13. Robert Adam: Drawing inscribed 'Candlestick for Sir Watkin Wynn Bart Adelphi 9th March 1773'. Sir John Soane's Museum

14. Soup tureen, gilt, one of a pair. James Young, 1778. Messrs. Lumley

15A. Adam Drawing, inscribed 'Sketch of a Turine for The Duke of Northumberland Adelphi 9th April 1779'. Sir John Soane's Museum

15B. Adam Drawing, inscribed 'Design of a Turine for His Grace The Duke of Northumberland Adelphi 4th March 1779'. Sir John Soane's Museum

16. Soup tureen, gilt, one of a pair. James Young, 1778. Messrs. Lumley

17. Soup tureen. Sebastian and James Crespell, 1771. Christie's

18. Coffee-pot. Charles Wright, 1776. Victoria and Albert Museum

19. Cup and cover. Louisa Courtauld and George Cowles, 1771. Victoria and Albert Museum

20. The Greenaway Cup (finial later). William Holmes and Nicholas Dumée, 1774. The Drapers' Company

21. Cup, cover and stand. William Holmes and Nicholas Dumée, 1774. Leeds Art Collections Fund.

22A. Cup and cover, gilt. William Holmes, 1775. Walker Art Gallery, Liverpool

22B. Cup and cover, gilt. William Holmes, 1776. Walker Art Gallery, Liverpool

23. Cup and cover, gilt. Thomas Heming, 1771. Trinity Hall, Cambridge

24A. Tea-urn. Nicholas Dumée, 1776. Christie's.

24B. Jug. Nicholas Dumée, 1777. Messrs. Lumley

25. Chocolate-pot. Henry Greenway, 1777. Victoria and Albert Museum

26. Tea-caddy. Louisa Courtauld and George Cowles, 1773. Victoria and Albert Museum

27A. Tea-caddy, gilt. Pierre Gillois, 1768. Victoria and Albert Museum

27B. Tea-caddy, gilt. Augustin Le Sage, 1777. Victoria and Albert Museum

28. Salver, gilt, one of a pair. Frederick Kandler, 1775. Museum and Art Gallery, Birmingham

81. Tea-urn. Hester Bateman, 1790. Courtesy, Museum of Fine Arts, Boston
82. Teapot and stand. Hester Bateman, 1782. City Art Gallery, Bristol
83. Teapot. Charles Aldridge and Henry Green, 1778. Mr. and Mrs. R. P. Kellett
84A. Cream jug. Maker's Mark S.H., 1790. Victoria and Albert Museum
84B. Tea-caddy. Henry Chawner, 1786. Mr. and Mrs. R. P. Kellett
85. Jug. J. Denzilow, 1781. Sir William Brooksbank Bt.
86. Jug. Charles Wright, 1778. Royal Scottish Museum
87A. Bougie box. Joseph Heriot, 1790. Dr. Kay Sharp
87B. Argyle. Henry Chawner, 1786. Private collection, on loan to the City Art Gallery, Bristol
88. Coffee-urn. Robert Hennell, 1788. Messrs. Bell
89. Jug. Thomas Daniel, 1790. Mr. and Mrs. R. P. Kellett
90. Cruet-frame. Hester Bateman, 1788. Victoria and Albert Museum
91A. d'Hancarville: William Hamilton's Collection, 1766–7. Vol. III, Plate 68. British Museum
91B. Cruet-frame, gilt. John Schofield, 1793. Earl of Lonsdale
92. Cruet-frame, gilt. John Schofield, 1789. Victoria and Albert Museum
93. Soup tureen. John Schofield, 1791. Christie's
94. Candelabrum, one of a pair. John Schofield, 1781. Mrs. Hiatt-Baker
95A. Candelabrum, one of a pair. John Schofield, 1794. Temple Newsam House, Leeds
95B. Pair of chamber candlesticks. John Schofield, 1791. Victoria and Albert Museum
96. Candlestick, gilt, one of a set of four. John Schofield, 1791–2. Earl of Lonsdale

CHAPTER I

Introduction: The Artistic Climate

There can have been few such complete revolutions in taste as that which took place between 1760 and 1770. Because taste, in this sense, is a collective thing—belonging to a class or a community rather than to an individual—it is easier seen in the decorative arts than in painting or sculpture where the artist's genius may be more apparent than the terms of the patron's commission. Of the decorative arts silverware has the unique quality of being made of a material which can be used again and for this reason to spend a lot of money on an avant garde object is not an irrevocable extravagance. This is one very good reason why silver chattels were so often in the van of taste and provided the models for objects of a less exalted substance. Looked at the other way round, many of the teapots, jugs and vases with which this book deals may represent the late eighteenth-century metamorphoses of lumps of bullion which started useful life as Elizabethan salts or Carolean porringers.

To put against this ephemeral quality of any object made of a precious metal is the fact that if its outward appearance might cease to be respected its substance remained too valuable to throw away. Through the centuries this has often meant that an object remains to us today because when it went out of fashion its owners, either through indolence or because they did not feel disposed to spend money on modernization, simply put it away in a safe place. Fortunately neo-classical silver has never appeared quite unacceptable to any generation with the result that there is a good deal of it still about in unspoiled state for us to deliberate over. In this it is unlike Adam's own work which went almost violently out of fashion during the second quarter of the nineteenth century, so much so that by the 1860's many of his most complete schemes had been rendered well-nigh unrecognizable in an attempt to make them acceptable to current taste.

Introduction: The Artistic Climate

From the craftsman's point of view the malleability of silver makes it possible to do nearly anything with it: a design by someone who had no working knowledge of the craft would probably need very little modification before being translated into reality. This has its snags for some of the worst objects ever made have been of silver faithfully following an inappropriate pattern. While this may be so it does not invalidate the proposition that a fine piece of silver may be the best ambassador of the skill and taste of its age. In the period under review most silver objects could also be made up in Sheffield plate thereby reaching a new class of customer whose standards inevitably contributed to current aesthetic values. The collective taste of the country therefore had a broader basis than ever before. In general solid plate was the prototype for the substitute, but not always so. Sometimes the designs that originated with the makers of plated wares had to be followed by the London silversmiths because they set a fashion. This cross-fertilization of ideas between different sections of the community was very noticeable by the 1780's in the simplicity and lack of ostentation of some of the best silverware.

One of the most remarkable things about the neo-classical period in England was its close connection with the work of one man—Robert Adam. So much is this so that we can reasonably talk about the 'Adam style' as being synonymous with it. Recent research suggests that neo-classical designs for furniture were first worked out in France[1] and that these helped Adam to crystallize his own ideas. In this context one must not forget J. F. de Neufforge's *Recueil élémentaire d'Architecture* as a published source of neo-classical forms for all manner of things over and above interiors and exteriors. It came out in several parts from as early as 1757 and no doubt provided foundation material for Adam to build upon. The important point is, however, that whatever lay beneath it he soon worked out a comprehensive and personal manner which was to influence European taste generally. It could be claimed therefore that by the mid 60's Britain was making her own contribution to fashion after centuries of being content to follow, often with consummate success let it be said,

[1] For detail studies on this subject see Svend Eriksen: 'Lalive de Jully's Furniture "à la grecque" ', *Burlington Magazine*, August 1961; Svend Eriksen: 'Marigny and "Le Goût Grec" ', *Burlington Magazine*, March 1962; Eileen Harris: 'Robert Adam and the Gobelins,' *Apollo*, April 1962.

German or Dutch or more frequently French initiative. An example of the last being the new techniques and feeling for proportion which the Huguenots brought over at the end of the seventeenth century, just when English silversmiths and their customers were looking for a fresh stimulus; some of the most satisfying silver ever produced was the result. On the other hand the rococo with its asymetrical extravagances, which was the next contribution from France, remained a foreign manner in England : it had to be watered down before it was generally acceptable. The Adam style could in a superficial sense be called a reaction against the rococo and within it certainly there was room once more for the things of which the English had shown themselves through the centuries to be particularly fond. Plain reflecting surfaces set off by carefully placed decorative textures or mouldings again played an important part. It would be a mistake to infer that during the neo-classical heyday artists and craftsmen did much more than glance backwards for inspiration; few of them were concerned with the real business of archaeology, knowledge of the past, but rather with creating a modern style along lines suggested by the achievements of the Ancients. Within the then current meaning of the term Adam was an artist of invention rather than merely an innovator, as he has sometimes been called. Because in the eighteenth century words had far more precise meanings than they do today—perhaps it shows a healthier attitude to be more sure of meaning than spelling—it is well to consider the accepted use of the word invention. Sir Joshua Reynolds typifies the educated man of his day and in his capacity as a Royal Academician he had teaching duties to the young. Duties which he took very seriously and his Discourses delivered before the students provide us with some of the best source material for the preconceptions of his period. He was concerned with definitions—aesthetic ones— which sets him well within the wider ramifications of the neo-classical movement affecting all Europe. In assessing the merits of artists of his own time and those of the past he discloses the basis on which his judgments were made. That they were so cut and dried, his meanings so carefully defined, makes them all the more valuable reading. In the sixth Discourse delivered in 1774 some of the most illuminating passages are to be found, an understanding of which is essential to our study if we are to apply appropriate standards. Reynolds says '. . . Invention is one of the great marks of genius; but if we consult experience, we shall find, that it is by being conversant with the inventions of others, that we learn to invent; as by reading the thoughts of others we learn to think . . .'. Later he maintains that 'The greatest natural genius cannot subsist on its own stock: he who resolves never to ransack any mind but his own, will soon be reduced, from mere barrenness, to the poorest of all imitations; he will be obliged to imitate himself, and to repeat what he has before often repeated'. There is a certain rhetorical element in all this and he certainly had a pedagogic axe to grind, but he sums his main thesis up later in the same Discourse by saying that '. . . he who has the most materials has the greatest means of invention . . .'. Although, especially in England, the idea of genius, the creative impulse, was developing, no one would have given the word its present connotation of indefinable greatness nor did invention suggest something unrelated to knowledge. In the eighteenth century knowledge was a necessity to the artist; the acquisition of it too would allow him to rise in the social scale. This point is well illustrated by the accepted hierarchy of subject matter; history painting was at the top because you needed knowledge—mainly of the classical authors—before you could start. Poor learned Stubbs was nevertheless at a disadvantage because of his overriding interest in animal rather than human figures. It will be remembered that he was not made a foundation member of the Royal Academy and his excursions into history painting were never very successful. The Fall of Phaeton was one of the few subjects with which he might have been expected, but as it happens appears not, to have felt at home. From all this we can see why Reynolds thought he was speaking for his generation when he said 'It is generally allowed that no man need be ashamed of copying the ancients: their works are considered as a magazine of common property, always open to the publick, whence every man has a right to take what materials he pleases . . .'. Ten years earlier Robert Adam in the introduction to his work on Diocletian's Palace[1] says 'The Buildings of the Ancients are in Architecture, what the works of Nature are with respect to the other arts; they serve as models which we should imitate, and as standards by which we ought to judge . . .'. This expresses substantially the

[1] *Ruins of the Palace of the Emperor Diocletian at Spalatro in Dalmatia by R. Adam, F.R.S., F.S.A., Architect to the King and to the Queen. Printed for the author, 1764.*

same view—Adam is concerned here specifically with buildings, but he was sensible that nature played an important part in the total effect of his own exteriors just as furniture and other movables did in his interiors. In short architecture was to him a comprehensive art.

To put against the apparently snobbish overtones of eighteenth-century artistic theory is the constant emphasis one finds on the idea of improvement; this is a vital element and quite unlike the romantic sense of progress current during the next century. Everything, it was believed, could be improved with a certain amount of effort—from nature to human taste. A necessary corollary of this was the assumption that the human mind was at the peak of creation and therefore had a right to dominate the rest of nature. Nature could in fact only be enjoyed when it had been adapted to the current idea of the beautiful—a Claudian pastoral— or the sublime—containing just the right amount of untamableness to tittilate the imagination and produce cold shivers down the spine. Capability Brown, the improver of landscape, was symptomatic. The significant thing is however that although the mind might represent the peak of creation it could nevertheless be improved. The man of taste was made not born. There is something basically democratic about this idea, and although in fact no one would have thought of putting it into practice below a certain level in the social scale, it was fundamental to the belief that the right models must be used for such comparatively cheap products as Sheffield plate and pottery. The consistency of late eighteenth-century aesthetic standards may be seen in, for example, the London squares and precincts made for different social strata; these have a unity which seems strange if we apply twentieth-century values. The difference between an object made for the rich and another aimed at the growing number of comfortably-off tradesmen was one of ornament or material but not of basic design. The catalogues issued by some of the Birmingham and Sheffield firms are good illustrations of this : teapots, candlesticks, or whatever it might be could be made up with or without ornament, in solid silver or in Sheffield plate. We shall look at this in more detail in a later chapter.

CHAPTER II

Robert Adam: The Composition of a Style

Taken *in toto* the Adam style was original and consistent. Seen separately many of its most characteristic motifs were already familiar; like all styles therefore which are based, however remotely, on the past—taken as it were from the dictionary of ornament—its novelty lay in a different way of looking at things. Just as words can change their meanings through the centuries, especially if used in fresh contexts, so patterns when recombined and given different emphasis may appear new. A simple illustration of this point is given by the wave ornament round the jug (Pl. 42) so typical of the Adam period yet quite as popular in its basic form with William Kent and his school.

Throughout the eighteenth century knowledge of classical civilization had been increasing. The Grand Tour which by the middle of the century had become a necessary finishing school for all males of gentle birth, and those aspiring to the consequences of it, did a very great deal to create a desire for knowledge. Archaeological digs such as those at Herculaneum and later at Pompeii were providing new information which suggested not only their artistic achievements, but how the Ancients actually lived and what they really liked to look at, in short their tastes and manners. The significance then of digging for data was that it disclosed domestic remains as opposed to public architecture. Temples for instance had always been visible to any traveller in the old world, but they might represent only what the builders thought acceptable to the gods, and these to the eighteenth-century gentleman whose essential reading included Ovid and Virgil were poetical fancies belonging to literature rather than life.

The publication of the findings at Herculaneum over the course of thirty-five years from 1757 was an undertaking of considerable consequence. The volumes provided the source for 'inventions' and their periodic appearance must have acted as a stimulant to patrons whose desires, by the usual process of demand and supply, filtered through to the craftsmen. The intention behind Martyn and Lettice's English summary was noteworthy for the authors saw their task as a kind of crusade, the object of which was to wrest from the selfish if not downright unworthy claimants information to which Englishmen had a birthright—Anglo Saxons were after all legatees of Greece and Rome too. In the preface they describe the difficulties put in their way by the Neapolitan authorities who saw the digs as an affair of state not to be meddled in by foreigners. Only part I of the translation was in fact ever issued—in 1773 —and this was enthusiastically awaited. Elmsley,[1] Matthew Boulton's bookseller, was one of those specially designated to act as agents; Boulton, Wedgwood and other manufacturers were subscribers as well as many of Robert Adam's most admiring patrons.

This more searching and critical view of the past led indeed to the publication of a whole series of fine books all of which followed a broad pattern: a quantity of engraved illustrations with a scholarly explanatory text and nearly always a strongly didactic purpose clearly stated. The Comte de Caylus's *Recueil d'Anti-quitiés* brought out during the 1750's and 60's is a case in point. Wedgwood for example, who particularly enjoyed browsing among books to educate himself, found it most illuminating and was only too willing to comply with the author's intention and allow it to influence the taste manifest in his own productions. The virtual 'discovery' of Greek vase painting as a source of inspiration to artists produced perhaps one of the most remarkable feats of book production of all time. The four illustrated volumes[2] describing Sir William Hamilton's collection, the beauties of which incidentally Wedgwood thought rather exaggerated in the plates, had a good deal of missionary spirit behind them. In the preface the author, d'Hancarville, makes clear what benefits he and Sir William believed they would confer on their contemporaries through this extremely expensive enterprise (Pls. 3, 43,

---

[1] Peter Elmsley (1736–1802). The well-known bookseller and friend of John Wilkes. His premises were opposite Southampton Street in the Strand and he was an agent for many of the lavish publications of the day.

[2] *Collection of Etruscan, Greek and Roman Antiquities from the Cabinet of the Hon^able Wm Hamilton His Britannick Majesty's Envoy Extraordinary at the Court of Naples*, 1766–7.

44, 55A and 91A) : 'we . . . have proposed to ourselves to hasten the progress of the Arts by disclosing their true and first principles, and it is in this respect that the nature of our work may be considered as absolutely new, for no one, has yet undertaken to search out what system the Ancients followed to give their Vases, that elegance which all the world acknowledges to be in them, to discover rules, the observation of which conduct infallibly to their imitation, and in short to assign exact measures for fixing their proportions, in order, that the Artist who would invent in the same style, or only copy the monuments which appeared to him worthy of being copied, may do so with as much truth and precision, as if he had the Originals themselves in his possession. It is by this means, that the present work may contribute to the advancement of the arts . . . ,' d'Hancarville goes on to say. 'We think also, that we make an agreeable present to our Manufacturers of earthenware and China, and to those who make vases in silver, copper, glass, marble etc. Having employed much more time in working than in reflection, and being besides in great want of models, they will be very glad to find here more than two hundred forms, the greatest part of which, are absolutely new to them; then, as in a plentiful stream, they may draw ideas which their ability and taste will know how to improve to their advantage, and to that of the Public.'

The silversmiths, Frederick Kandler or Matthew Boulton for instance, might be said to have invented in the same style; they were after all working in a different medium and without colour, while Wedgwood, as a potter, was concerned to beat the Ancients on their own ground—to make 'Greek' pots technically more perfect than real ones, to do in fact what the Greeks might have been expected to have done if they had had the benefits of living in the eighteenth century. Wedgwood dearly wanted to prove his success by placing his copies alongside the originals for all to see. The distinction between inventing and copying—both morally and aesthetically acceptable—is made quite plain in the passages quoted, as is the intention of the book to be a source of patterns. It is interesting to note that Sir William's collection was soon bought by the British Museum which thus became the first public gallery—in 1772—to exhibit Greek pots. Some forty years later the Elgin marbles were bought in the pious hope that they might inspire an artistic renaissance in England comparable to that of sixteenth-century Italy. By this time the idea of a museum as a source of moral as well as aesthetic benefit had become established.

Lord Burlington's generation had been content to go to Palladio or Serlio for its classical models, and certainly such a comparatively modern work as Degodetz's *Les Edifices Antiques de Rome*, published in 1682, was a source book much in demand. While on the grand tour Robert Adam, like the good Scot that he was, fell to considering what profitable work he might combine with his studies and it was not without significance that he hit upon the idea of bringing Degodetz up to date. By that he meant making it more accurate by remeasuring the buildings and providing perspective views to give an impression of what the monuments actually looked like. In the end he threw up this work setting himself an easier task, the success of Wood and Dawkins' *The Ruins of Palmyra* no doubt influencing his decision. This book, published as early as 1753, and its companion volume *The Ruins of Balbec*, which came out some four years later, were to prove two of the richest repositories of ornament for the craftsmen of the neo-classical period (Pls. 2, 4A, 4B and 5). Mrs. Montagu,[1] herself an arbiter of taste, was well aware of the inspiration behind many of the rooms she admired on her rounds of visits. She specifically mentions for instance that some of the ceilings at Bowood came from *Palmyra* and Adam himself was to draw freely on this source, in particular at Osterley. The ceiling of the Drawing Room is a good example, for he took it directly from a soffit in the Temple of the Sun (Pl. 5 top), and although the architect transformed the central roundel into an oval and played with the feathers, he used much of the detail unaltered. Wood and Dawkins (the latter is said to have spent £50,000 on the publication of both volumes)[2] travelled mainly to satisfy their own curiosity as they readily admit, but it seems churlish to discount what is said in the preface, that some of '. . . the most remarkable places of antiquity on the coast of the Mediterranean might produce amusement and improvement to themselves as well as some adantage to the publick'. It is unlikely that they were less aware than de Caylus or d'Hancarville of a vocation to improve taste.

The ruins at Palmyra are remarkable on a number of counts.

[1] See Chapter V, pp. 60–62.
[2] See T. M. Clarke: 'The Discovery of Palmyra', *Architectural Review*, March 1947.

Most important for our present purpose is the marked local variation on the classical norm. The work of the native school of carvers, which delighted in the deep undercutting of capitals and the rich interiors of some of the tombs in which the background to the ornament on the ceilings was coloured, is a case in point. Although the expedition did no digging and therefore observed only what was standing, the picture of the ancient city with its colonnaded streets and the gilded bronze capitals catching the sun was indeed a rich one. That Robert Adam found the subject of the book so intriguing was partly, we might guess, because it represented a legitimate precedent for just those variations on a theme, or 'inventions', of which he was to prove himself such a master. While he did not hold a high opinion of Wood, who he thought pretentious, he was prepared to pay lip service to his work at Palmyra and Balbec calling it '. . . one of the most splendid and liberal . . .' undertakings '. . . ever attempted by private persons' (he includes Dawkins and Bouverie—who died on the journey—in his panegyric). He says this in the introduction to his own volume on the palace of the Emperor Diocletian. This was to be the published fruit of Robert's grand tour, though in fact with the help of Clérisseau he spent much more time and labour in measuring up the Baths of Diocletian and Caracalla. Adam saw the relevance of domestic architecture to his own career and justified his choice of the palace for attention when he wrote '. . . nor could I help considering my knowledge of Architecture as imperfect, unless I should be able to add the observation of a private edifice of the ancients to my study of their public works. . .'. All the schemes of study which he pursued with such perseverance on this prolonged educational trip yielded a repertoire of forms and ornament which was to last for the rest of his days.

Personal contacts were of great importance in forming Adam's character as a designer. His very fortunate meeting with Clérisseau in Florence led to a relationship which not only provided him with an exacting artistic mentor who could help with his researches on ancient buildings, but with a go-between able to introduce him into that avant garde circle in Rome where neo-classical theories were being formulated. It was here that he met Piranesi who, incidentally, was to enjoy enormous prestige in Britain even to the extent of being made a fellow of the Society of Antiquaries. Expectedly the young architect was impressed nearly as much by the great man's volatile personality as by his work, at this time of mainly archaeological significance, and learnt much from him. Ten years later Piranesi published *Parere su L'Architettura*; this book is of prime interest in our context because of its new emphasis on the imagination—taking motifs from all the ancient civilizations to create a modern style. It fits in very well with Robert's views that rules were unimportant compared with the 'beautiful spirit of Antiquity'. This tossing aside of rules was of course an anti-classical attitude but one that was at the root of Adam's genius.

The controversy which ranged round the question of whether the Greeks or the Etruscans or the Romans should be given the most credit for ancient art and architecture had little practical consequence in the eighteenth century. It will be remembered that the full effect of Stuart and Revett's *Antiquities of Athens*, the major part of which was not published until 1788, was to be felt in the nineteenth century when it was associated with the reaction against Adam. It did not really make much difference that Adam insisted on assumming that the vases that he thought so much of were Etruscan or that Wedgwood called his new works Etruria rather than Greece—the former sounds more interesting anyway. What did matter was the fact that the writings of men like the Comte de Caylus, Winckelmann or Le Roy were read and suggested new fields of study and decorative sources as well as theories. In point of fact Robert was by nature omnivorous in his tastes and it is amusing to recall that, in an age when correct taste was so important and the standards by which it was judged still rigid, such a characteristic was of very dubious merit. His liking for Vanbrugh and the romantic solidity of romanesque buildings was not shared by most of his contemporaries for example, and Clérisseau once admitted to James Adam that he thought Robert's taste was at times worryingly unorthodox.

Adam's personality and his social aspirations are of great interest; he was what we would call today a go-getter with an acute mind which took him all the way, especially when backed by a team of brothers equally determined that he must make his mark. This aspect of the Adam phenomena must not be overlooked for without it there would have been no Adam style for decorative artists to follow. The family's ability in public relations ensured that Robert worked for the richest in the land and by a snowball process it was they as much as the architect himself who created a fashion for all things 'Adamatic', as Soane called it.

If one analyses the shapes and individual motifs that went to make up the style—the swags, the rams' heads, the paterae, the husks, or whatever it might be—the ultimate sources from which they derive are usually not very difficult to find. The classical urn or vase shape became a sort of trade mark of the period; it proved itself highly satisfactory for hollow-ware of most kinds from race cups to hot-water jugs and was a useful motif in two dimensional schemes. That Greek pots should provide the main prototype shapes was appropriate. They in their time had been designed to be useful, their clean contours and decoration that made no attempt to deny the plane of surface were valued by their original owners for whom they must often have represented the limit of acquisitive aspiration. Pots were a major Greek art and one which must always have been relatively cheap and therefore popular. They had survived in considerable quantity and variety to inspire an age part of whose major contribution to the arts was in inexpensive materials such as pottery and Sheffield plate and which had new means of quantity production at its finger tips.

If Greek vases suggested many of the current shapes, the repetitive and flowing designs upon them, and occasionally the figures also, provided endless ideas for decorative schemes (Pls. 3, 43, 55A and 91A). We have seen something of the contemporary admiration for these examples of classical art in the history of Sir William Hamilton's collection and its publication in book form where the decoration upon the vases is shown in flat projection. Adam himself says somewhat naively perhaps 'That the Romans must have been well acquainted with this taste during the whole course of their greatness is almost certain, from the vast number of beautiful vases and urns which have been found in every part of Italy within these three centuries, and which now adorn both the public collections and the private cabinets of the curious all over Europe'.[1] That these vases had been absorbed into Roman art provided further sanction for the working hypothesis that ornament from different sources might successfully be worked into a new visual language.

The Adam brothers were proud of their so-called Etruscan style

[1] *The Works in Architecture of Robert and James Adam*, Part I, Vol. II, 1779.

and they wrote this about Derby House: '. . . although the style of the ornament, and the colouring of the Countess of Derby's dressing room, are both evidently imitated from the vases and urns of the Etruscans, yet we have not been able to discover, either in our researches into antiquity, or in the works of modern artists, any idea of applying this taste to the decoration of apartments.' They say they have consulted 'Montfaucon, Count Caylus, Count Passeri, Father Gori, and the whole collection of Antiquarians who have treated of those matters, without finding a single circumstance that hints at, or alludes to, any such style of decoration'.[1] They seem most anxious to assert that they were the first to invent such a novel form of interior adornment and that it was based upon particular ancient sources. Reading between the lines one might suppose that they were worried lest someone should recall William Kent's decorations at Kensington Palace and Rousham and draw the conclusion that Raphael's and da Udine's work in the Vatican Logge and the Villa Madama inspired both. Kent was too near in time to be an admissible influence, but of the brothers Robert particularly had the greatest respect for the genius of renaissance artists partly because they had the advantage over his generation of living two centuries earlier when it might reasonably be assumed that ancient buildings were less ruinous and therefore easier to study. They provided indeed a sort of link between him and the classical world.

It will be seen that Adam drew on a very wide range of sources from Greek vases and Roman tombs to renaissance palaces and yet his was one of the most consistent and easily recognizable styles ever to be fashionable. Within it too there was plenty of room for individual idiosyncrasies among the craftsmen who provided the objects to go in the magnificent interiors. Such people did not need to travel, for their inspirational needs were well provided for, if not by actual designs of the master himself, then by the many archaeological-cum-pattern books of the time. The splendours of the neo-classical period are indeed best judged now by the decorative arts which remain. Soane, although he was critical of Adam on many counts, summed up the situation well in a lecture given before the Royal Academy students in 1812 when he said, 'The light and elegant ornaments, the varied compartments in the ceilings of Mr. Adam, imitated from Ancient Works in the Baths

[1] Ibid.

and Villas of the Romans, were soon applied in designs for chairs, tables, carpets, and in every other species of furniture. To Mr. Adam's taste in the ornament of his buildings and furniture we stand indebted, inasmuch as manufacturers of every kind felt, as it were, the electric power of this revolution in Art.'

CHAPTER III

London Made

Neither Robert Adam nor his brother James appear ever to have been commissioned by a silversmith to do a design, but they did produce quite a number of drawings for silver to the order of their aristocratic or wealthy patrons. Some of them were for pieces like race cups which might be said to have had an entity of their own, others—the larger group—were for silver which would take its place on sideboards and dining tables as part of the decoration of the room. We know how anxious Robert was that his interiors should be complete and not spoiled by discordant elements, and, as we shall see, at one time an attempt was made to persuade Matthew Boulton at Birmingham to make suitable silver and other metal-work in his manufactory at Soho. From the Adams' point of view Boulton had just the mechanical and technical means at his disposal to further the cause.   1356842

The Adam drawings which Sir John Soane bought in 1833— some eight thousand of them—were those remaining in their London office after the deaths of the brothers. They give a very good idea, in their range of subjects, how all pervading was the Adam style, and in their various states of completion, from rudimentary sketches to finished drawings, how mere suggestion could be dashed off or the smallest detail calculated. There are a number of drawings clearly for silverware and others which may have been. Unfortunately not many can be linked with existing pieces, but among those which can is that, signed by Robert Adam, of about 1763 inscribed 'Vase for Thomas Dundas Esqr for a Prize' (Pl. 7). Another drawing (Pl. 6) was either discarded in its favour or meant for a second cup. The race cups made from the first drawing are splendid examples of the magnificence expected in such prizes at this time. It is worth having a critical look at one of them, the Richmond cup of 1770 by Daniel Smith and Robert

Sharp (Pl. 8) who, incidentally, had made what was probably their earliest version in 1764 for Hugh Percy, Earl of Northumberland.[1] The former cup is inscribed within the foot rim 'Wm Pickett, London Fecit 1770' suggesting that this silversmith, though not the maker, was the retailer and wanted his name to be associated with it. One might recall that Pickett's partner, William Theed, retired in 1768 leaving this well-known firm under the one name until Pickett took Philip Rundell into partnership four years later. By the late 80's the firm had become Rundell, Bridge and Rundell, a business association made famous by Paul Storr and the extravagance of the Prince Regent.[2] If we compare this cup with the drawing it will be seen how very close they are. Nevertheless something vital has been lost in the translation, the drawing has an elegance lacking in the cup, the shape of which by comparison is lumpy; this is made more apparent by the lower foot, presumably an attempt on the part of the silversmith to make the spiral effect more telling when seen from above. On the whole the decoration has been made bolder and less fiddly by increasing its scale and therefore reducing the number of elements in a given length. Robert was so apt to overdo his decorative motifs and here is an interesting case of a very able silversmith adapting and improving upon the work of the master; it is curious that he was not more sensible of shape. The theme of the frieze is followed fairly closely (Pl. 9), so are the caryatid handles which are strangely reminiscent of the tea-kettle by Charles Kandler in the Victoria and Albert Museum of some forty years earlier. The craftsman, however, received no guidance in filling the two cartouches; in the event they contain bas-reliefs of racing scenes practically identical with those to be found on other pieces, for instance the Doncaster race cup of 1786 (Pl. 68). They were almost certainly stock designs, and cast from the same moulds, any slight difference between them being due to the chasing-up and finishing. What silversmith made the original moulds is a matter of conjecture, but we do know that Smith and Sharp supplied miscellaneous silver to Wakelin and Taylor whose mark appears on the Doncaster race cup. Smith and Sharp indeed were leading makers who

[1] See Charles Oman: 'English Silver at Burlington House', *Burlington Magazine*, January 1956.
[2] For further details on Wm. Pickett see N. M. Penzer: *Paul Storr*, B. T. Batsford, 1954, pp. 69-72.

enjoyed the patronage of the discerning rich. Pls. 1 and **78** show other examples of the very high quality of their work.

Among the drawings made for objects which would become part of the decoration of a room one of the most carefully finished and exactly stated is that for a candlestick (Pl. 11A). This design had healthy progeny; a number of candlesticks that follow it closely were made by John Carter in 1767—a pair of them, part of a larger set, is now at Temple Newsam House, Leeds (Pl. 10). Others were made by Sebastian and James Crespell in 1769, maybe to add to the earlier set. The drawing suggests that the base should be round and it is tempting to think that the silversmiths had decided by their own 'ability and taste' that it would have been better square. In fact Robert himself—or perhaps James —seems to have come to this conclusion for there are detail drawings (Pl. 11B), which may have been afterthoughts, showing the circular trumpet standing on a square plinth—substantially similar to the candlesticks as made.

The Crespells worked increasingly for the firm of Parker and Wakelin from 1769 onwards and by 1782 they may have done so exclusively. Unfortunately it is in the records missing at Goldsmiths' Hall that one might expect to find information about Carter such as his apprenticeship and other personal data. He probably had family as well as business connections with Smith and Sharp and he was certainly one of the leading silversmiths of the day. The plate bearing his mark—he specialized in candlesticks and salvers —is usually of high quality and the designs he used were often in the van of taste. It is worth noting here that he was one of the witnesses who gave evidence before the House of Commons Committees against Birmingham and Sheffield being empowered to have their own assay offices. Indeed he had a vested interest in what went on in these provincial centres for he, like some other Londoners, sold Sheffield candlesticks under his own mark (see page 85).

In the same general category, but obviously intended to play a larger part in the garniture of a room, are a set of four candelabra of 1774, also bearing the mark of John Carter (Pl. 12). They are taken from an Adam drawing dated March 9th 1773, for Sir Watkin Wynn (Pl. 13). Mr. Ralph Edwards[1] suggests that

[1] Ralph Edwards: 'Torchères and Candelabra, designs by Robert Adam', *Country Life*, 23 May 1947.

some fine tripodal candle stands (now in the Victoria and Albert Museum) which are related to Adam sketches of 1777 and were made for the eating room at No. 20 St. James' Square, may have been intended for use with the candelabra on special occasions. It will be remembered that No. 20, which Robert built for Sir Watkin in the early 1770's, was one of his most successful town houses. The tripod became a symbol of antiquity which caught the neo-classical imagination; as early as 1756 the Comte de Caylus had advocated the 'invention' of variations on the tripod theme and designers like James Stuart and, much more, Robert Adam were making use of it within a few years. It proved indeed particularly suitable for 'lights' and their accessories and, rather obviously in view of ancient usage, cassolets of all sorts, as well as for two dimensional decoration, for example Stuart's design of 1759 for Spencer House.[1] The drawing for the candelabra, like that for the candlesticks discussed earlier, is well presented, but gives far less detail. It is interesting here to see how the silversmith has both simplified and elaborated the basic design. The final form is more workmanlike, the festoons and especially the drops would have been very vulnerable, and the central shaft almost impossible to clean. A good example, in fact, of a design by someone who had no idea of the limitations, or indeed qualities, of the medium in which it was to be carried out. One must admit, however, that the candelabra in the drawing is a most beautiful object and that its more practical interpretation seems to lack the vital spark, appearing pedestrian by contrast. On the other hand the detail, that on the candle-holders for instance, has been worked up with consummate success.

The tureens bearing the mark of James Young (Pls. 14 and 16) are based on very rudimentary sketches (Pls. 15A and 15B), but with enough suggested to give a pretty good guide to the silversmith. There is no drawing for either of the salvers on which the tureens stand, and indeed in neither case do they seem quite to fit; the fussiness of the floral motifs is out of keeping with the simpler of the two designs and similar embellishment only adds confusion beneath the very elaborate feet of the other tureen. The proliferation of ornament giving the encrusted effect, so characteristic a feature of the silver made up from Adam designs,

[1] See Svend Eriksen and F. J. B. Watson: 'The Athénienne and the Revival of the Classical Tripod', *Burlington Magazine*, March 1963.

is in both tureens set off by large areas of plain surface. The magnificence of the whole is made greater by gilding. One feels rather that it was only when there was not time to finish a drawing that it is ever suggested that any space should be left unornamented. It is an amusing thought that this 'Victorian' characteristic went so unappreciated in the nineteenth century; no doubt the Adam spectacle was too recent. On the other hand the English silversmith seems in all ages—even when fashion was at its most flamboyant—to have had an instinctive appreciation for the beauties of the metal unadorned. It is noteworthy that both the tureens share the same design of lid. By the time they were made Birmingham and Sheffield had for some years blatantly, but effectively, used the same parts in different combinations to produce original effects.

Some of the best Adamite silver was made without the direct agency of Robert at all, by inventing in the manner of the Ancients, using often the same sources as he did, and indeed seeing through similarly conditioned eyes. Silversmiths could not be anything but men, or women for that matter, with a feeling for their material and the traditions of their craft, and so in a subtle way they made the Adam manner into a silver style. Charles Wright's work is instructive in showing a craftsman's approach to changing fashion. He was the maker of so many of those transitional coffee-pots which attempt to make the best of both worlds by retaining a certain rococo swing within an acceptably neo-classical shape (Pl. 18). One can guess that these would have appealed to the not-so-fashionable customers. Wright cannot be dismissed too lightly, however, for some silver bearing his mark is far from ordinary; the race cup (Frontispiece), comfortably within the new idiom, is full of original touches by comparison with which the very orthodox laurel swags and paterae in the middle section seem weak. The racing scene—a similar cartouche on the other side is blank—is very like one of those on the Richmond race cup though it differs in detail.

To Louisa Courtauld and George Cowles neo-classicism seems quickly to have become a natural way of expressing themselves as artists. They had an extraordinary knack of using a charming variation on a familiar motif in just the right place and of contrasting an area of decoration with the most complimentary amount of plain surface. The cup of 1771 (Pl. 19) shows off their skill very well. The eye delights in the flowing frieze, every other flower in which is reversed with its stem making an extra spiral in the design; the frilliness of the acanthus leaves is subtly emphasized too by the reflecting powers of the plain convexity of the cup. The foot, incidentally, which here fits so well into the general design, is almost identical with that of the Richmond race cup and could well have been taken from it. It is not surprising that plate of fine quality should bear a Courtauld mark and it is clear that Louisa took over a great deal more than tools and patterns from her husband Samuel when he died in 1765. The Courtauld family have been well-written-up[1] and a fair amount is known about them; only two bearers of this illustrious name were active in our period, Louisa and her son Samuel II. After her widowhood Louisa carried on the business until, in 1768, she took George Cowles into a partnership which lasted for nine productive years, ending when Louisa was joined by her son. This arrangement did not last long, for in 1780 the business was sold up, so ending the connection of the Courtauld family with silversmithing. Cowles, who after 1777 worked on his own, was himself steeped in the Courtauld tradition for he had been one of Samuel I's two apprentices, the other being Stephen Dupont of Huguenot stock. A few months after his master's death he was made free by service 'with the consent of Louisa Perina Courtauld, the widow and Extrix and on the testimony of Robert Sharp Goldsmith and Daniel Smith Merchant Taylor'. He got himself still further tied up with the family by marrying Judith Jacob, a grand-daughter of Augustine Courtauld. This, indeed, made him a nephew of Louisa. From their first coming over here there was a strong sense of community among the Huguenots which, though born of necessity, lasted long after they had become integrated with the social and economic life of their adopted country and had lost any definable special characteristics as silversmiths. Nevertheless during the second half of the eighteenth century many of the best makers bore Huguenot names, and no doubt their long association with the craft had a lot to do with it. Francis Butty and Nicholas Dumée, for example, were certainly in the top flight. A few years later some splendid plate emanated from what must have been a comparatively short working partnership between Dumée and William Holmes. The somewhat flamboyant Greenaway cup (Pl. 20) incorporates one

[1] See S. L. Courtauld: *The Huguenot Family of Courtauld*, London 1957.

version of those curiously realistic serpent handles so much in vogue in the middle 70's and which seem to have been a speciality of theirs. Another cup (Pl. 21), also of 1774, uses the same handles; it is one of the most elaborate pieces these makers produced and incorporates every conceivable type of decoration from heavy three-dimensional castings to French type flat-fluting—the latter being an early use of this mannerism in England (see page 72). The bas-reliefs of racing scenes on either side of the cup are very like those on the Richmond and Doncaster race cups, but as in the case of the cup by Charles Wright they differ in detail. One of the most unusual features of the piece is the detachable stand, the main purpose of which seems to be to add visual weight at the base. Obviously considered a masterpiece in its day it, like the Richmond cup, bears the name of its retailer, this time a somewhat obscure silversmith with no known mark who inscribed the bezel of the cover 'Wᵐ Moore fecit Paternoster row London'. On the two cups of 1775 and 1776 (Pls. 22A and 22B) which bear Holmes' own mark, serpent handles have been carried to their logical extreme. The jug of 1777 (Pl. 24B) by Dumée also sports a fine variation on this reptillian theme. All three pieces are in fact very similar in conception and belong to a group of objects drawing their immediate inspiration, it would seem, from Wedgwood's Jaspar ware—the alternate matted and burnished stripes being the silversmith's equivalent of the coloured bands. Here is an unusual instance of silver design following ceramics, in this case the pottery that was modish at the time.

The classical urn shape, as we have seen, proved very adaptable for so much of the hollow-ware of the period; it was of no consequence that the prototypes were mainly ceramic—rarely metal, let alone silver. While there need be no particular link between utility and design in the case of race cups and other purely decorative pieces, jugs, caddies and tureens, provided the ratio of capacity to overall size was not unreasonable, could easily take an urn form too. Knowledge of actual objects excavated from sites like Herculaneum and Pompeii, apart from the published engravings already discussed, did filter through to the craftsmen. Real things are likely to be more titillating to the imagination than somebody else's distillation of them and it looks as though one may have been the starting point for the chocolate-pot by Henry Greenway (Pl. 25). Its surface decoration, even so, is closely related to motifs illustrated in Wood and Dawkins' *Palmyra*—possibly the same engraving that inspired Adam for Osterley (Pl. 5 top) and the source of the circles linked by leaves round the waist may have been suggested by an illustration in d'Hancarville's book (Pl. 43).

Many objects in regular demand were not susceptible to urn forms and had therefore to be thought out from scratch, very often with excellent results. Such things as salvers, wine-coolers, candlesticks, cake-baskets and, perhaps rather strangely, teapots come into this category. The last had gradually established such a strong tradition that even in the most fashionable circles they were accepted as being exempt from more than a passing reference to the current idiom. This could no doubt be explained by the fact that tea was still very much associated with the East; it had not lost its exotic character and Cathay had psychological connotations the reverse of classical. Tea-caddies, though they might be urn-shaped, were quite often made in the form of miniature tea-chests, one by Louisa Courtauld and George Cowles (Pl. 26) being a good example of how the eighteenth century could mix its aesthetic metaphors with charming results. Chinese characters are engraved on three of the sides while the fourth bears a neo-classical crest, all of them and the top being bordered by a formal pattern very much more Greek than Chinese. The silver-gilt caddies by Pierre Gillois (Pl. 27A) and Augustin Le Sage (Pl. 27B), two more good Huguenot names incidentally, employ a simple cube shape to good effect, but are embroidered all over with symmetrical patterns of a very occidental kind. By the time the second was made the neo-classical repertoire had hardened into a grammatical visual language.

Commissioned, one suspects, primarily to contribute to a display of opulence is a pair of gilt salvers by Frederick Kandler (Pl. 28); these are certainly among the most satisfying pieces of their kind. As in the cup already appraised (Pl. 19), they depend for their effect on the contrast between plain surface and embellishment with the added interest of contrasting techniques—the salvers are indeed show-pieces of silversmithing skills. Of the same date, by the same maker, for the same patron—to judge by the armorials—is the wine-cooler (Pl. 29). This is a remarkable piece too, this time for its boldness and basic simplicity; the suggestion of movement inherent in the band of wave pattern, emphasized by the contrasting verticality of the reeding on the body and the leafy base, points to great self-confidence and originality of mind on the part of the maker. It is a pity that the armorials on this piece have obviously been added to a design not intended for them and look most uncomfortable. A third example of this silversmith's imaginative powers is the jardinière (Pl. 30). There is nothing even superficially neo-classical here and, while a porcelain form no doubt lurks somewhere in its aesthetic ancestry, there is a strangely art-nouveau touch about it. Kandler came of a gifted family of German origin which probably had connections with Johann Joachim Kaendler, the modeller of the Meissen figures. His elder kinsman, Charles Kandler, was the maker of the famous Jerningham wine-cooler[1] and the magnificent tea-kettle and stand in the rococo manner in the Victoria and Albert Museum. Frederick, who as a silversmith did not use his first name Charles, presumably to prevent confusion, was very prolific and produced outstanding work in this earlier style too, as can be seen from the Hervey silver at Ickworth.[2] He first registered his mark in 1735 and it is remarkable that forty years later he had the vigour which, added to his experience—or should one call it eye—enabled him to produce some of the most interesting plate of the Adam period.

The Adamization of cake-baskets was a comparatively simple matter. Like soup-tureens they were traditionally oval in form and so were among the forerunners of a shape which became fashionable for almost every sort of object in the 1780's. By simplifying the decorative elements, paying more attention to the proportional relationships of foot, handle and body, and by adapting simple neo-classical patterns for the piercing, an object could be produced which epitomized the fashionable manner. Pls. 35A and 35B show very good examples of this sort of treatment. Like baskets, epergnes—which might be thought of as proliferations of baskets —were easily clothed à la mode. There are many fine ones still in existence suggesting that they remained popular, and inevitably significant, pieces of dining-room plate in spite of Mrs. Montagu's comment in a letter, written in 1776,[3] that she had been told epergnes were out of fashion. That by Thomas Pitts (Pl. 36) made some time after the letter was written was certainly intended for a

[1] See N. M. Penzer: 'The Jerningham-Kandler Wine-Cooler', *Apollo*, September and October 1956.
[2] See N. M. Penzer: 'The Hervey Silver at Ickworth', *Apollo*, February and April 1957.
[3] Mrs. Montagu to Matthew Boulton, 8 April 1776.

fashionable customer. Another good example is that of 1777 (Pl. 37B) by the same silversmith. Thomas Pitts, father of William, who was also responsible for some fine epergnes and baskets, was one of the specialists who seems to have made little else, judging by the number which bear his mark and by the ledgers of Parker and Wakelin recording Pitts' supply of epergnes to them. That shown in Pl. 37A, bearing this firm's mark, was most likely made by him or his son. The firm, already referred to in connection with the Crespells, had moved into the first rank before our period and continued to hold its position right through the nineteenth century under the title of Garrard and Co.; it was Garrards who succeeded Rundell, Bridge and Rundell as Royal goldsmiths. Parker and Wakelin sold some of the best neo-classical plate to an impressive list of customers, their output (Pls. 31 and 38) being supplemented, as we have seen, by the work of leading craftsmen employed by, or producing silver for, them. Among these incidentally was Matthew Boulton of Birmingham. To avoid confusion it may be helpful here to list the names under which, successively, the firm flourished during the second half of the eighteenth century, as follows: Edward Wakelin (the first of his name to be associated with the firm, his mark was entered in 1747); John Parker and Edward Wakelin (their mark being found on plate from the early 1760's); John Wakelin (son of Edward) and William Taylor (their mark entered in 1776), and John Wakelin and Robert Garrard (their mark entered in 1792).

At the beginning of the Adam period the London silversmiths were in a good position; they had no rivals and were highly skilled in the traditional methods of their craft. Early in the century they had resented the presence of the Huguenot refugees—the 'necessitous strangers' who were not only willing, because of their circumstances, to work for less reward, but who brought new skills at once attractive to potential customers and hard to learn. The next challenge to the supremacy of London came, as we shall see, from the upstart towns of Birmingham and Sheffield in the 1760's and represented the first technological revolution in this most ancient of all crafts.

Before we leave London to see what was happening in the Midlands it should be noted that although the Assay office at York reopened in 1776 this did not amount to a further claim for attention from the provinces; rather it was the answer to a local

need and was brought about largely by one go-ahead firm—
Hampston and Prince. They supplied at most a regional demand.
The silversmiths of Newcastle-upon-Tyne, Exeter and Chester
were not aiming at the London market either and were in no way
rivals to their brethren in the capital; some of the increase in the
volume of work going through the Assay office at Chester during
the late 60's and early 70's was caused by one or two Birmingham
makers.

CHAPTER IV

Birmingham and Sheffield I:
A Revolution in Method

T he rise of Birmingham and Sheffield as major centres of silversmithing during the last forty years of the eighteenth century was an important event in the history of taste, quite apart from its interest to the economic historian. Ever since the end of the Marlborough wars, early in the century, prosperity had increased as Britain's place in Europe became more settled. A greater sense of security, too, worked its way down the social scale producing conditions favourable to the growth of a solid and self-conscious middle class. Appropriate possessions were needed and those charming country-made versions of fashionable furniture are good examples of how social aspirations could be met in a very practical way. Whether decorative, useful or both, silver chattels had always been high on the list of status symbols, and with the invention of Sheffield plate, on the face of it indistinguishable from the real thing, together with the use of new and labour-saving techniques, Birmingham and Sheffield brought them within the reach of the not-so-rich. In short they were able to meet the increased demand when it was most pressing. By the early 1770's these towns were producing, as well as fused plate, some of the best silverware of the day. They also had in common most of the technical innovations for which they were renowned; but here the similarity between the two, on the whole friendly, rivals ends.

The background to the trade in each place was quite different. Birmingham had for centuries been a metal-working centre, especially of brass, but owing to the absence of trade corporations it is not easy to define who made what, for often one man combined several trades. By the middle of the eighteenth century, however, there was already a tradition of making toy wares in the precious metals, including the staple buttons and buckles. Sheffield from remote times had been the centre of the cutlery trades, which were very much more specialized than those of Birmingham; today the flourishing Company of Cutlers in Hallamshire in the county of York, to give it its correct title, is the only remaining livery company outside London. In the early days of silver and plate production nearly all the workmen were taken from the cutlery trade, and as late as the 1770's the Cutlers' Company was complaining that its members were not only leaving the trade, but were teaching indentured apprentices to make silver and plate at the expense of cutlery.[1] There was more work than there were men to do it, and we can form some idea of the situation from a letter written by Samuel Roberts to a local newspaper in 1843, which Bradbury[2] quotes at length. Roberts was a member of one of the leading families in the business. He says, reminiscing about his father's time, around 1765, when the production of plated goods was already considerable, that 'the trade was completely new in Sheffield—where no similar goods, of any metal, had been made and workmen at all qualified to manufacture them had to be sought for from London, York, Newcastle, Birmingham etc. . . . Therefore during the first 40 years the journeymen platers were, as a body, the most unsteady, depraved and idle of all other workmen'. He goes on to explain that the employers took a firm stand and the quality of the work-people soon improved. The reasons he gives for this are interesting and may be summarized as follows : wages were high compared to those of other workmen; whether trade was good or bad, prices paid for making remained constant, so did prices of goods sold; young children were not employed and apprentices rarely taken under fourteen. This last meant that they were 'respectably educated', moreover they were expected to bring a premium of £20 or two years board—all of which suggests that masters could afford to be choosey. Roberts says too that disputes between masters and men were few and adds, rather pointedly, that the Sheffield manufacturers from the first thought it in their interests to keep up the quality of their goods and induce had workmen to go elsewhere—to Birmingham perhaps where inferior things were made for abroad. As early as the 1760's one of Boulton's objects was to deny the disgust implied in the word

[1] See S. W. Turner : 'The Establishment and Development of the Silver and Plate Industry in Sheffield', *Apollo*, December 1947.
[2] F. Bradbury : *History of Old Sheffield Plate*, Macmillan 1912, pp. 40–41.

'Brummagem' already being used for many of the products of his town. While it would be suitably cautious to take what Roberts says with a pinch of salt—he was after all writing to a newspaper long after the days he describes, and was a member of a flourishing Sheffield firm—circumstantial evidence suggests that his statements were substantially true. In Sheffield there were many firms producing the same high class of goods, if in a rather limited range, and often, as we shall see, the output of one was indistinguishable from that of another. In Birmingham Matthew Boulton and his works at Soho were unique. Certainly there were a number of toymen producing good work, but this was of a different order, for in the early 1770's silverware was virtually limited to small stuff like buttons, buckles, sugar-tongs, snuffers and the like. The Birmingham specialities such as vinaigrettes, snuff boxes and caddy-spoons were not made in any quantity before about 1800.

Clearly it was a problem to train and keep really good workmen, and an exchange of letters late in the century between Boulton and Roberts, Cadman and Co. illuminates not only the particular problem, but an enlightened attitude, shown by one of the correspondents at least, to industrial relations. It is salutary to remember this in the light of nineteenth-century abuses; Boulton's firm writes from Birmingham as follows :

'Sirs,

Permit us to inform you that we are and always have been desirous of preserving a friendly intercourse with the Sheffield Manufacturers of Plated Wares; and have in consequence avoided giving any Temptation to induce any of their Workmen to quit their employ : well knowing that such conduct would be productive of much inconvenience to each Party, besides the vexatious disputes that would naturally occur, and ultimately cause a retaliation; and not only so, but it would tend to encourage bad principled and ungrateful Men to move from Shop to Shop and in other respects to use their Masters ill.—

We persuade Ourselves that your good sense and honourable principles make it unnecessary for us to enumerate : or dwell any further upon the pernicious effects that would result from such impolitick Conduct.

We therefore beg leave to assure you we shall adhere to the Principles we profess and in return we flatter ourselves that you and the other Gentlemen of Sheffield in this line of Business, will also continue to act upon the like Plan : and not in any instance take a Workman without a written discharge.—Our present reason for addressing you on this subject arises from the late conduct of Thos. Troth one of our Workmen, who has quitted our service without any reasonable Cause. He served his Apprenticeship at Soho and has been chiefly employed in mounting.—

We have also reasons to believe any offers he may have obtained from you or other Houses have originated from his own application, and we trust, and hope, that neither you nor anyone else, will give him any Encouragement for obvious reasons.—

We have likewise been informed he had made application to Messrs. Holy, Wilkinson & Co. and Messrs. Fenton, Creswick & Co.—in consequence we beg you will present our Compliments to these Gentlemen and shew them this Letter, or acquaint them with the tenor of it, and in return we shall be ready to render you any Service in our power.

Remaining most respectfully,

Sirs,

Your obedt. hble. Servants.

Soho near Birmingham
the 3 Oct 1799'

To which this reply was received :

'Gent^m.

We are this Day favoured with yours of the 3rd inst. In answer we have to observe that we trust we are amongst the last to use any unfair means to entice the Workmen of any other manufacturer to leave them—but we must confess that we think the Rule which you lay down as proper to be observed viz, not to take a Workman in any instance without a written discharge from his Employer, would be neither just to Master nor Workman—we conceive every Man who is neither contracted nor indebted to his Master is at perfect liberty (private obligations out of the question) to embrace any opportunity which occurs of benefitting himself—otherwise a Worthy Man and good Workman who should be so unfortunate as to be employ'd by an unprincipled Master might be prevented from ever employing his talents either to his own advantage or that of the public—in short, it would be giving that unlimited power to the Masters that few would be able to use with moderation and it would be imposing that degree of vassilage upon the workman which would completely damp every spark of emulation—we must confess ourselves rather surprised at hearing from you at all upon the Subject as we never in our lives had any communication with any of your Workmen, all that we know of the present Business is that about a Week ago we recd. an anonimous Letter from Birmingham saying that if we wanted Workmen there were two (one of them the person you mention) who would be glad to serve us and desired an answer but as we entertain but an indifferent opinion in general of those who leave their native place in search of employment we took no further notice of the Letter than to write to a Friend to make some enquiry respecting them to which we have as yet received no Answer—we cannot close this without embracing the opportunity of expressing our desire of an open Friendly communication whenever circumstances render it necessary either for information or explanation— and We trust that you will always find us to have pursued that conduct which in a change of situations we should approve of in others towards us—we must beg your excuse of this scrawl as it is wrote in haste—we are

With Sincere esteem,

Gentm.

Your Humble Servants,

Roberts Cadman & Co.

October 9, 1799
We shall take care to forward your Letter to the Houses which you desire.'

Some doubt is thrown on the genuineness of the sentiments expressed in Boulton's first paragraph, however, by another letter written some fourteen years before by John Hodges, the manager of the silver and plated goods department of Soho, to Boulton who was away from Birmingham at the time. After telling his employer how pressed they had been of late and desperately in need of more 'plated workers' he says 'Mr. Chamberlain has again written to Sheff^d to procure hands and we thought it advisable to offer £5–5 to any good workman to bear his expenses here—In the course of time there is little doubt of being able to obtain some

Good hands . . .'.[1] Perhaps time had altered Boulton's views—or more likely the pressure of his needs.

Be this as it may it is certain that Boulton made every effort to cater for his own requirements and his manufactory at Soho, quite apart from what it produced, was a monument to the organizing ability of its presiding genius. In a letter[2] written to James Adam on October 1st 1770 he says that he has '. . . seven or eight hundred persons employ'd in almost all those Arts that are aplicable to the manufacturing of all the metals the simi metals and various combinations of them, also Tortois shell, Stones, Glas, Enamel, etc., I have almost every machine that is aplicable to those Arts I have two Water mills employ'd in rolling, pollishing grinding & turning various sorts of Laths. I have train'd up many and am training up more young plain Country Lads all of which that betray any genius are taught to draw from whom I derive many advantages that are not to be found in any manufacture that is or can be establish'd in a great & Debauch'd Capital. I have likewise establish'd a Correspondance in almost every mircantile Town in Europe Which regurlary supplies me with orders for the groser & Current Articles which enables me constantly to employ such a number of hands as yields a Choice of Artists for the finer Branches and am thus enabled to errect and employ a more extensive & more convenient aperatus than would be prudent to errect for the finer Articles only'. The country lads he speaks of were probably fatherless children, parish apprentices and the like for whom he built and furnished a house. That he taught the promising ones to draw shows what importance he attached to his design department. He seems to have treated them well and inspired genuine loyalty. He disliked the usual practice of premium apprenticeships and refused quite large sums; no doubt he felt that a greater sense of dedication to their work would be shown by boys who owed much to him. This letter is significant for the general information it gives and even more because it is Boulton's own statement of what he is most proud of after the Soho factory had been established some eight years. His father, Matthew Boulton senior, had been a fairly typical Birmingham toymaker, producing mainly buckles. He died in 1759, his son inheriting the business; it

[1] John Hodges to Matthew Boulton, 6 March 1785.
[2] Quoted by H. W. Dickinson: *Matthew Boulton*, Cambridge 1937, pp. 60–62.

was not long before the latter's plans for the future were laid and with thoroughness put into effect. In 1762, so that he would be free to organize and supervise production, he took John Fothergill into partnership to look after the mercantile side of the business. Although, as Boulton himself suggests, the bread and butter work was intended to carry the 'Fine Wares' he needed the fortunes of both his wives to keep him solvent and the precarious financial position of the firm eventually preyed on the mind of Fothergill who was certainly not the right sort of partner for the ebullient Boulton.

In an age, however, when mechanical contrivances which could reduce handwork were looked upon with respect—machines not yet being seen as usurpers of human rights—Boulton was soon able to make Soho one of the sights of the country. It was visited by some of the most influential people of the day, and proved a highly successful advertisement. This open house attitude taken by Boulton was novel and certainly paid dividends. Mrs. Montagu whose favour was of much consequence in the best circles, wrote to Boulton in 1777 saying : 'You have rendered the Town of Birmingham important and honourable to this kingdom. Your manufactures are a great national object and have been of infinite utility in rendering our Commerce flourishing during our contest with America. . . .'[1] Admittedly her letters are a little effusive and she was a relation of Boulton by marriage, though this fact, considering that he married his deceased wife's sister, might well have prejudiced her the other way.

One of the most fascinating things about Soho must have been the variety and ingenuity of its products and the fact that very few commissions, however difficult, were ever turned down. There were occasions, nevertheless, when an order had to be refused, usually because time could not be given to it, or because suitable workmen were too busy already. This seems to have happened more frequently towards the end of the century when Soho had become well established as the source of fine quality products, even though by this time Boulton had turned his attention to other things and their design often lacked inspiration. Two passages in a letter written by Richard Chippindall, the agent in London, to Boulton are illuminating. He complains of having to turn down orders for hash dishes etc. 'because the time they take at Soho is

[1] Mrs. Montagu to Matthew Boulton, 4 April 1777.

more than double to that of Sheffield—indeed nearly treble—I have been looking over & find since Xmass last the Orders for those very Articles which we have been Oblig'd to *refuse*—are more than Double the number of those we have executed, & when it is consider'd that those who we refuse must of course go to a more expeditious market—nay what is worse—perhaps necessity drives them to send down one of our Own Dishes or Covers to Sheff'd as patt'n to go by . . .'. Further on he says '. . . & as I have repeatedly been inform'd *good* hands are not to be had—surely there is a fair Opening for *good machinery*—& if I was to tell our friends, they were at Sheffield in possession of a machine of which Mr. M. Boulton's manufactury cou'd not boast on acc't of the *expense of erecting*—my veracity wou'd certainly be much question'd—or the Character of Soho injur'd'. The letter is dated 22 May 1792.

This brings us back to Sheffield and the question of what machines could be used in the making of silver. Although Sheffield plate as such does not come within this book's terms of reference, the subject must be touched upon for two reasons. In the first place nearly every object made at Sheffield or Birmingham at this time could either be made up in silver or the cheaper material. While on this subject it will be recalled that Matthew Boulton, until about 1770, was one of the very few manufacturers of fused plate on any scale outside Sheffield itself; further, throughout our period he was almost certainly the biggest single producer of it. In the second place some of the machines that proved most useful were tried first in, or found necessary to, the manufacture of fused plate. Not very long after its invention in Sheffield the development of the industry was greatly accelerated by the use of die stamping. This meant that a run of thousands of, say, candlestick parts, which had then only to be assembled, could be turned out quickly and cheaply. When this technique was applied to silver thin sheet could be used which had been rolled on the flatting mills, invented earlier, but now in their heyday; rolled silver was in any case less liable than battery silver to split when raised in high relief. Much depended on the cutting of these dies to ensure a clear impression, but Sheffield men knew steel and were adept at it: recent improvements in the making of the steel itself helped a good deal too. One wonders whether die-stamping would have been used so soon and so effectively had it been possible to cast fused plate. The limitations of the material certainly put a premium on technical innovation. There was for instance the problem of piercing, for this could not be done by fretsaw, the normal method for the silversmith, without breaking away the silver and exposing the copper. The fly punch, however, was exactly the machine required, for the enormous pressure it exerted to punch a pattern out had the effect of burring the silver over on both sides and so concealing the copper core. With careful use intricate open-work patterns could be produced in solid silver, as well as plate, which rivalled in finish and of course surpassed in regularity the best handwork (Pl. 34). Then there was the swage block, a recent invention, which made easy the production of silver ribbon of any contours on one side. This had many applications including the strengthening of the rims of thin silver hollow-ware of all sorts. Matthew Boulton, from his earliest days in his father's business, had been fascinated by the idea of technical advance and sometimes his letters remind one of our own attitude towards the wonders of space travel—one can almost see the vistas opening before him when he thought of improvements that could be made. One might take the parallel a little further, for nowadays it is only when concerned with the conquest of space—or perhaps the depth of the sea—that we view applied science and mechanics as aids to a non-economic object, the attainment of which will be judged in terms of 'progress' or 'national prestige' whatever the contemporary variation in terminology may be. Boulton's object was to make his fine wares as perfect and as plentiful as he could. He was a world away from the squalid idea that only the market matters, not the product, which lies behind modern factory mass-production of indifferent goods. Detail mattered to him enormously—he was one of those people—but there was more to it than this, for his products, within his own terms of reference, were works of art and it was part of the maker's job to see that they did not easily lose their integrity. This idea lies behind an interesting letter to Lord Shelburne in which he says: 'It is almost impossible to make some things of silver *very elegant* unless there is contrast of *Colours*, viz., bright burnish'd parts contrasted with a beautiful white Dead Matt, but as such Matt is difficult to be clean'd, so people in general have chosen their silver Ornaments pollish'd in every part. Now as I could wish to see every elegance introduced into the Plate Manufacture, I therefore shall endeavour to obviate that common objection against dead work in Silver, by furnishing every Person with the Apparatus, and the knowledge of Cleaning the Dead parts as well as the Bright polished. When I have prepared the materials and Printed the Necessary Directions (which will be before your Lordship's Candlesticks want Cleaning) I will send them for the use of your Lordship's Silver Scullery.'[1] One can imagine the effect of traditional butlers' methods on anything so easily spoilt. The mat effect was clearly a significant element in the decoration of many Soho pieces. For an important commission some ten years later, which appears to have been sent abroad, a tin-lined case was advised particularly to preserve the 'dead mated part'.

Even when he was not the inventor of a particular process Boulton was often able to improve it. A case in point is the draw-bench. This ancient principle of drawing metal through tapered holes to make wire was used at Soho to produce silver wire of consistent thickness and texture inviting use for objects such as the basket (Pl. 33B), in its way a technical *tour de force*. Of a different artistic order, but of interest in this context, are the small wire baskets with glass liners popular as sugar-bowls in the 1770's. These were often decorated with thin stamped leaves and flowers with wire tendrils, all soldered on. One, of 1773 (Pl. 33A), although it bears London marks was probably made in Sheffield (see p. 84). With these modest productions in mind it is fascinating to examine the charming cake-basket made by Richard Mills (Pl. 32). Superficially this might well have been made with the aid of all the machines discussed, but closer examination reveals that the main body is all in one piece, having been worked up from the sheet. The three dimensional effect of the corn ears, the bows, and 'wire' is all given by repoussé work, and the piercing has been done with the fretsaw. The handle and the rim are cast. This basket indeed is a masterpiece of traditional skills and may well represent a conscious attempt to out-do machines.

[1] Matthew Boulton to the Earl of Shelburne, 7 January 1771. Quoted by Arthur Westwood: *The Assay Office at Birmingham*, Part I.

CHAPTER V

Birmingham and Sheffield II:
The Provinces Established

I t is now time to consider Boulton himself as a phenomenon and
what he, as one of the personalities of the time with the means
of production at his fingertips, contributed to the neo-classical
image.

By way of introduction it should be remembered that during the
second half of the eighteenth century some of the most original
brains of the day lived in Birmingham or within striking distance
of it. It was a free-thinker's Mecca in every sense, not only
religious, and those who made the pilgrimage often found it to
their liking. Joseph Priestley, who came in 1780, said: 'I consider
my settlement at Birmingham as the happiest event in my life,
being highly favourable to every object I had in view, philoso-
phical or theological. In the former respect I had the convenience
of good workmen of every kind, and the society of persons
eminent for their knowledge of chemistry, particularly Mr. Watt,
Mr. Keir, and Dr. Withering. These, with Mr. Boulton and Dr.
Darwin (who soon left us by removing from Lichfield to Derby),
Mr. Galton, and afterwards Mr. Johnson, of Kenilworth, and
myself, dined together every month, calling ourselves the Lunar
Society, because the time of our meeting was near the full moon.'[1]
Moonlight was an important consideration to those who lived at
any distance. Unfortunately for posterity the Society kept no
records—its meetings were intended for informal discussion and
the cross-fertilization of lively minds. Boulton, Erasmus Darwin
(Grandfather of Charles Darwin the naturalist), and Dr. William
Small, friend and tutor of Thomas Jefferson, founded the society

[1] Quoted by Eliza Meteyard: *The Life of Josiah Wedgwood*, Hurst and
Blackett, 1865–6, Vol. II, p. 558, from J. T. Rutt: *Life and Correspondence of
Joseph Priestley*, 1831–2.

about 1766 and it only faded out with the deaths of the main characters, who included John Baskerville the printer, Samuel Galton and James Watt; among the visitors were Josiah Wedgwood, John Smeaton, Sir William Herschel, Sir Joseph Banks and almost everyone who might contribute something to discussion and who happened to appear within orbit. Probably the thing they all had in common was the belief that they represented the vanguard of discovery heralding a new sort of improvement in the lot of mankind. Few of them were learned in the sense of being well grounded in classical literature and language. Boulton we know found this a handicap, and Wedgwood was a tireless self-educator.

In the late 60's these two men were considering whether they might be of mutual benefit to each other; they were almost the same age and were already leaders in their respective fields. There is an interesting correspondence between them and one of the subjects discussed was the best way to advertise their wares— particularly on the continent. Boulton was obviously helpful here because he was well aware of foreign competition, especially from France, one of his objects at this time being to produce better ormolu than the French did. It was Boulton who in 1767 first suggested to Wedgwood that the latter should issue catalogues with engraved illustrations. His agents abroad, as we shall see, had the two-fold commission of selling goods, and incidentally the whole idea of Soho, and sending back material that might be useful to model from. Boulton proposed that Burslem should produce vases, etc., which could be mounted at Soho; the antique trade was doing well at the time and there was such demand that even, as Wedgwood put it in a letter to his partner Thomas Bentley in 1768, 'old China bowles, jarrs etc. are mounted in Metal' and, one might add, sold for high prices. It is surprising that more did not come of this scheme, but the clue may lie in the character of Boulton, the fecundity of whose ideas was such that they could not all mature, and the suspicion of the much more conservative minded Wedgwood. Another passage in the same illuminating letter[1] reads '. . . he (Boulton) proposes an alliance betwixt the Pottery and Metal branches, viz. that we shall make such things as will be suitable for mounting, & not have a *Pott* look, & he will

[1] Josiah Wedgwood to Thomas Bentley, 21 November 1768. Quoted by Meteyard: op. cit., Vol. II, pp. 96–98.

finish them with the mounts. What do you think of it? Perhaps you wo^d rather he wo^d let them alone. Very true, but he will be doing, so that the question is whether we shall refuse having anything to do with him, & thereby affront him, & set him of doing them himself . . .'. Wedgwood often went to Soho and the two men liked and respected one another; the potter was sensitive about rivals, however, and was probably apprehensive about what Boulton might be up to next—he says of him in another letter to Bentley some months later: 'I like the man—I like his spirit—He will not be a mere drivelling copyist like the antagonists I have hitherto had. . . .'[1]

At this point we may bring the Adam brothers on the scene again. They, just as much as the other two, felt themselves besieged by plagiarizers. In a letter to Boulton, James says 'You cannot imagine with what rapidity some patterns that we gave, to oblige some of our friends, for grates & other little articles of Furniture have run thro' the shops—nay they come to D^m Yard (Durham Yard, The Adelphi) & Copy Doors chimney pieces & Ceilings etc without our being able alltogether to prevent it'.[2] Boulton's silverware was copied during the time it was away being hallmarked in Chester, and Wedgwood wrote desperately to Bentley that '. . . there is nothing relating to business I so much wish for as being released from these degrading slavish chains, these mean selfish fears of other people copying my works'.[1] No one likes being imitated, at least without acknowledgment, but there is more to it than that in the case of all these men. So much depended on quality in the building up of the neo-classical ideal—just the thing a plagiarizer invariably ignores.

Robert Adam and his brother James, who did most of the practical business of this great fraternal partnership, were in constant need of craftsmen who could on occasion carry out their designs and better still, in view of their business commitments, make things in the Adam manner. As far as furniture was concerned they had what they wanted in Samuel Norman, William France, and above all Thomas Chippendale. Boulton and Wedgwood in their own fields seem to have been just what the brothers were looking for. Now, one idea for the new Adelphi precinct,

[1] Josiah Wedgwood to Thomas Bentley, 27 September 1769. Quoted by Meteyard: op. cit., Vol. II, pp. 212–216.
[2] James Adam to Matthew Boulton, 5 November 1770.

which but for Scottish cannyness might well have proved financially disastrous, was to encourage suitable manufacturers to rent show-rooms for the display of their goods : a sort of design centre in which the commodities on sale would receive the unofficial imprimatur of the architect himself. In the early 70's the brothers exchanged lengthy and informative letters with Boulton on the one hand and Wedgwood on the other in which the pros and cons of providing show-rooms for them were discussed. These letters give a good idea of the sort of public aimed at and indeed the shrewdness of the parties concerned. Nothing came of it all for various overt reasons, mainly concerned with capital outlay, the tying-up of stock and management difficulties. It all boiled down, however, to the fact that both Wedgwood and Boulton were satisfied that they could do what they wanted to do rather better from their provincial fastnesses.

It is clear from his correspondence that Boulton, apart from commissions for ormolu fittings for houses like Osterley, from time to time received Adam drawings for silverware to work from. Evidence of what sounds like a worth-while commission, for example, is contained in a letter of 1775 from Thomas Coutts the banker, who, on behalf of the Earl of Findlater, sends 'three designs of Mess. Adam for Terrines'. His lordship was among those who thought highly of Boulton and consulted him about a number of things—including steam-engines. He seems to have been prepared to help in a practical way by putting Boulton in touch with useful people in Paris. They evidently discussed French neo-classical silver and the work of the much admired Robert-Joseph Auguste comes in for comment in a letter written from Soho in 1776. Boulton says '. . . I w'd have Elegant simplicity the leading principal whereas in my opinion such of the Orfèvre of the French as I have generly seen is troy Chargè. But as I have not seen any of the best productions of Monsr August I therefore presume I have seen nothing, His fame I am persweded is founded in superior Merit because I have heard so many Noblemen of good Tast concur in ye same opinion of him—I therefore am desirious of availing myself of your Lordships good Offices at Paris in ye spring . . .'.[1] It might be added that Auguste's patrons in England included the King. Boulton was also in touch with that most indolent authority James Stuart who sometimes

[1] Matthew Boulton to the Earl of Findlater, 20 January 1776.

supplied drawings or advice when the occasion demanded—he seems to have had a hand in the Admiralty tureens (see pp. 81–84). James Wyatt took an active part the in design of Soho silver for a number of years[1] and Sir William Chambers was another architect whose designs were sometimes used.

Boulton's main sources, however, appear to have been classical objects in the collections of his friends and patrons; small sculptures of various sorts sent him from abroad or supplied by sculptors like John Flaxman the elder, and engravings and illustrated books often found for him by his agents. Among these patrons—they included for instance the Dukes of Richmond and Northumberland, Lords Shelburne, Dartmouth and Cranbourne—were some of the richest and most intelligent connoisseurs of the time and most of them seem to have been interested in what Boulton was doing. There is an amusing passage in a letter quoted from earlier in which Wedgwood says 'Mr. Boulton & I go a curiosity hunting all day tomorrow. We begin with a visit to Ld Shelbourne, & shall then proceed—the Ld knows where, for I cannot yet tell you. Mr. Cox is as mad as a March Hare for Etruscan Vases, pray get a quantity made or we shall disgust our good customers by disappointing them in their expectations'.[2] Further on Wedgwood says '. . . Mr. Boulton has not yet sent any of his things to St. James's. He soars higher, & is scheming to be sent for by his Majesty! I wish him success . . .'. It is worth recording that he did later receive a direct commission from the King as well as being received in audience. This was obviously written in amusement, but it does pinpoint Boulton's social aspirations which are by no means without significance to his work. He certainly fancied himself in the sort of society the door of which was open a chink to him. Some of his projects, such as clock-making, had definitely grandiose overtones and his ormolu and fluorspar creations were often enriched to the point of flamboyance.

Mrs. Montagu, already referred to, was an important figure in his career for she could provide a personal link with the right people. She will be remembered not only for her letters and

[1] See E. Robinson: 'Eighteenth Century Commerce and Fashion: Matthew Boulton's Marketing Techniques', *The Economic History Review*, Vol. XVI, No. 1, 1963.

[2] Josiah Wedgwood to Thomas Bentley, 21 November 1768. Cox was a dealer who specialized in porcelain.

writings such as her attack on Voltaire in 'An Essay on the Writings and Genius of Shakespeare' but also because she made her house the meeting place of the intellect and fashion of London. Wyatt worked for her at Sandleford and she commissioned James Stuart, who incidentally she found 'idle and inattentive', to design Montagu House at the corner of Portman Square for her. The correspondence with Boulton is full of interest. In a letter to her of January 1772, Boulton says '. . . ye present age distinguishes it self by adopting the most Elegant ornaments of the most refined Grecian artists, I am satisfy'd in conforming thereto, & humbly copying their style, & makeing new combinations of old ornaments without presuming to invent new ones'[1]—a very telling passage in the light of late-eighteenth-century aesthetic theory. Boulton was pleased to borrow as models things he admired in Mrs. Montagu's house—their ownership underwrote, as it were, his own judgement. She agrees to lend him some silver perfume-burners or cassolets and in a letter of October 1771 says of them that she will '. . . be vain of claiming any share of what comes from Soho. I hope when you are in Town you will do me the favour to dine with me, and then you will be sensible how agreable the aromatick gales ("sweet gale" or bog myrtle) are from these Cassolettes when they drive away the Vapour of soup & all the fulsome savour of dinner'.[2] We learn that they made their entry with the dessert. In a further letter she enlarges on the subject thus : 'I hope you will not imagine that I pretend to give Mr. Bolton a pattern, an athenian in the best age of the arts could only be worthy to furnish him with a model but there is a prettiness of fancy in the Cassolettes which improved into grace & good taste w'd render the sort of thing a beautiful addition to a table.'[3] How interesting it would be to know more about these pieces which she believed Boulton might so well improve upon. One might guess them to be French, both from her spelling and the fact that such things were fashionable across the Channel at this time. Soho may have been the only English source of them. Boulton obviously supplied Mrs. Montagu with quite a lot of things from Soho. She asks on one occasion if he has 'any kind of writing standishes that

[1] Matthew Boulton to Mrs. Montagu, 16 January 1772, quoted by E. Robinson : 'Matthew Boulton, Patron of the Arts', *Annals of Science*, Vol. 9, 1953.
[2] Mrs. Montagu to Matthew Boulton, 31 October 1771.
[3] Mrs. Montagu to Matthew Boulton, 9 January 1772.

are not very expensive',[1] on another she writes, April 1776, 'I wish to talk with you on the subject of making me a Service of Plate. I should never invite more than a dozen or thirteen guests, rarely so many, therefore 9 dishes for each course with Tureens for Soup, and a suitable number of plates would be sufficient. For Soup I should use china plates. My Tureens must not be very large nor the dishes of the first magnitude.'[2] Pertinent to dining fashions is a letter written by another of Boulton's correspondents nearly seven years before. He says 'I have enquired amongst those who have nothing to do but to copy or invent new modes of luxury & magnificence, & who have lived amongst ye French, who understand these things best of any nation, about ye idea we had conceived of a Service for a Dissert—à là grec—but I find that China only or perhaps in some instances Glass; is thought proper for fruit & confectionary & that nothing of metal, as we thought of, wou'd be conformable to ye present *whim* of Tast'.[3] Finally on the subject of Mrs. Montagu a letter about various objects supplied nicely sums up Boulton's respect for her views. He says, talking about a 'Tea Vase with Dolphin spouts' which he originally intended for her: 'as it did not come up to my expectation, I therefore have finish'd two others which shall be deliver'd to you about this day week and beg you will take that which you like best—I will make any alterations in any of them but what wou'd please me most wou'd be to work after your own design by which I am sure to proffit even if I lost money by it.'[4]

Over a long period of years Boulton bought prints from Alderman Boydell, an intriguing character best remembered today for his Shakespeare Gallery and the commissioning of artists to fill it. One order sent to William Mathews, Boulton's agent, in May 1771—'Please go to Boydell and buy 2 or 3 prints of running Horses with Jockies on their backs the best that you can get, we want 'em to model from'[5]—may have had something to do with the Thetford Cup. The specification for this runs as follows : 'The cup to be made without handles. Three horses running on one side

[1] Mrs. Montagu to Matthew Boulton, 31 October 1771.

[2] Mrs. Montagu to Matthew Boulton, 8 April 1776.

[3] Thomas Pownall, M.P., to Matthew Boulton, 8 September 1769. Pownall was sometime Governor of Massachusetts and author of *The Administration of the Colonies*.

[4] Matthew Boulton to Mrs. Montagu, 14 December 1772.

[5] An order to William Mathews, 10 May 1771, quoted by E. Robinson: op. cit., *Annals of Science*, Vol. 9, 1953.

on the other, a medal as you propos'd with the inscription, Thetford Cup / run for in 1771, & won by / Lord Clermont Stewart. To be sent to His Grace The Duke of Grafton Arlington Street before ye 1 day of July & not to exceed sixty guineas.'[1] The cup did not arrive when it should have done and Boulton wrote the following letter making his excuses to the Duke. Some of the writer's difficulties at this stage in the history of Soho are so clearly evoked that it is worth quoting in full : 'I was favour'd a few Days ago with a letter from Ld Clermont expressing his surprise & chagrin at finding the Cup for Thetford Races was not deliver'd in time and desire'd I would explain to your Grace the cause of it—In consequence of which I take this liberty—My orders were to deliver the Cup by the 1st July. I proceeded accordingly and when the Cup was nearly made it was by the carelessness of one of my workmen melted in soddering on of some ornaments (a misfortune that will happen sometimes even to the carefull)—Another Cup was made directly but was delay'd many days at Chester, where we are obliged to send everything to be essay'd & mar'k'd wch is a greivence that will prevent us (unless removed) from ever establishing an extensive Manufactory of Silverwares upon such a footing as will be most advantageous to this Kingdom, however in spight of the aforesaid delays the Cup was finish'd and sent from this place the 30th of June expecting it would have been left at yr Graces House in London on the first of July but upon information of our Clerk in London that the Cup was not arrived by the Stage Coach led me to discover that the Coach being over loaded the proprietors thereoff had delay'd (untill their next journey) taking ye Cup, which was the real cause of its not being deliver'd on the 1st of July and of much Vexation to myself

It was the first Vessel of silver ever made in my Manufacture & therefore was not so perfect as I could not make another which I should be happy to convince your Grace of on some future occasion.'[2] The reference to the cup being the first vessel of silver made at Soho is curious. He may have meant the first important commission rather than that his silverware had literally been confined to toys and candlesticks until now. When it was finished the cup cost £52 10s. 0d. The excuse of inexperience implied

[1] An undated note.
[2] Matthew Boulton to the Duke of Grafton, 1 August 1771.

here was made directly over the Admiralty tureen finished a few months later (see p. 82).

As evidence that Boulton supplied ormolu mounts to at least one of the leading furniture firms of the day is a series of letters written to Ince and Mayhew. One of these, dated August 26th 1771, refers to volumes of the *Museum Florentinum* being used as a source of designs and patterns. Boulton did not then possess the work and he asks if he may borrow it for Soho or alternatively '. . . we sh^d be much oblidged to Mr. Ince if he would order for us at our Booksellers (viz: Mr. Elmsley in the Strand) such of the Volumes of the Museum Florintina as he thinks will be usefull to us, there being many Vol^s in that work that will be of little use & we know not the particulars of it'. This massive publication was issued in Florence in the 1760's on the treasures of the city. It covers pictures as well as statuary and gemstones, many of the commentaries being written by the scholar A. F. Gori, but as it was profusely illustrated by engravings, Boulton's lack of Italian would not have been a serious handicap. Some two months later a postscript in a letter addressed to Elmsley reads: 'Along with the 5 volumes of the Herculinium [the Antiquities of Herculaneum referred to on p. 26] you will receive some other Books which are also to be bound, and I beg you would loose no time to procure me the 1. 2 & 3 Vols of the Museum florentine.'[1] So Boulton clearly thought it worth having the relevant parts of this work permanently to hand in his design department.

A few years before, Wendler, Boulton's agent in Italy, wrote from Venice about various things he had bought for his employer. He says '. . . I have been in Naples and Subscribed in Your Name & for Yr Acc't, for ab't 456 prints in folio divided in 4 volumes; the first will appear in ab't 2 or 3 weeks, & th' other Successively in about a years time with an english & Italian explication of the ancient Etrurian Vases, fitt to furnish 2 or more rooms & to chuse from the said Prints handsome Designs & patterns for the Birmingham Manufactorys. It is reckoned a fine piece of work as being printed with colours imitating the Said vases. . . . Knowing You a Lover of Such kind of Curiositys; I thought I cou'nt do wrong to Subscribe for the same';[2] Boulton replies saying that he

---

[1] Matthew Boulton to Peter Elmsley, 2 October 1771.

[2] P. Wendler to Matthew Boulton, 4 July 1767. This refers to d'Hancarville's volumes on Sir William Hamilton's Vases.

would be delighted to have the prints and, referring to a figure of Venus Wendler had bought for him, says 'as to Statuary & Painting I never durst buy any as very fine pieces come to more mony than is suitable to my purse & if they are not fine they are worth nothing at all & give me more pain than pleasure'. The letter ends: 'Mr. Fothergill is hunting in ye Northern parts of Europe whilst you are in ye South, but I hope ere tis long we shall all meet in good health.'[1]

An analysis of Boulton's silverware certainly suggests that d'Hancarville's volumes on Sir William Hamilton's Vases proved the most useful of his source material. The three jugs (Pls. 41, 42 and 45) are based on the traditional ewer shape of classical times, used by silversmiths from the Renaissance onwards. The Greek prototype for the handles is unmistakable (Pl. 44), and may indeed have been taken from this very illustration. Pergolesi's *Original Designs*, issued at intervals between 1777 and 1801, were useful to him too. An engraved sheet by Pergolesi, published in 1782 (Pl. 46) and now stuck in one of the Boulton pattern books (see p. 81) may have influenced the design for the tureen (Pl. 47 top left). This in a sense refers one back to Adam himself for Pergolesi was associated with the architect in the decoration of such houses as Syon and played a considerable part in the dissemination of the Adam manner. Allocating the various decorative motifs to their respective sources is an amusing exercise; a perusal of Pls. 41 and 42 with a reference to Pl. 43 gets one a long way. The important thing, however, is the final product. The consummate skill with which the various elements are combined to create objects each one of which if seen in isolation would not suggest that other equally satisfactory permutations were possible. The Boston jug (Pl. 42) probably suffers most in the photograph as the parcel gilding is lost—it is in fact perhaps the most impressive of the three. Candlesticks, because the basic form could be divided into three pieces, holder, shaft and base, were no doubt the easiest objects on which to get effective variation by the simplest means. Those illustrated (Pls. 50, 51A and 51B) are all good designs both aesthetically and functionally; the base or foot on the candlestick (Pl. 51A) is, incidentally, identical with that on two of the jugs and there is a similar link between the candlestick (Pl. 50) and the cup (Pl. 52).

[1] Matthew Boulton to P. Wendler, probably July/August 1767.

An interesting light is thrown on the limits imposed by Birmingham and Sheffield methods of production in a letter written in 1775 by Boulton to Robert Mylne, the architect, with whom he was on very friendly terms. He says: 'I like your drawings of Cand^ks better than our own, yet small as the difference is it will require a new sett of Dyes to conform to your drawing and if we make a new set of Dyes it w^d be more occonomy to make quite a new pattern which I should be happy to do after one of your designs. However I will send you a patt^n of Cand^ks made as near to your drawing as the present dyes will permitt at the same time I will send you drawings of 2 New Cand^ks which we are upon the brink of compleating and must beg you'l take your choise.'[1] It is a curious thought that the idea of building up objects of prefabricated parts and decorative elements, not new in principle then, is still familiar today, when it is degraded to make a spurious brand image between say the same motor car made in different factories. In the final analysis we may find ourselves in substantial agreement with late-eighteenth-century aesthetic standards. The visual success of the best neo-classical products can be credited in the first place to the excellence of the decorative motifs taken from the Ancients, which after all had in most cases been gradually improved and refined by centuries of craftsmen, and in the second place to the selective skill, and belief in what they were doing, of men like Boulton, Wedgwood and Chippendale.

It would be a mistake to think however that, for example, Boulton's work always met with approval. Harsh things were said about him—and to him—and there seems to be no doubt that he had occasional lapses. The Duke of Richmond was not at all pleased with some candlesticks supplied from Soho. In a letter dated July 4th 1773 he complains bitterly about them, saying that not only were they the wrong size 'but the greatest Defect is in the Capitals, which are exceedingly coarse and ill finished, even worse than the most common of the Sort which may be bought in London, whereas I expected by employing you to have had them very neat'. He appears to have got little satisfaction—it is difficult to make out who was the more at fault—and on July 19th he wrote again, this time a letter which must not only have hurt Boulton's creative pride, but cut him to the quick by the social slight inferred. The Duke says, referring to the candlesticks, 'I am sorry to find you

---

[1] Matthew Boulton to Robert Mylne, 4 November 1775.

make any tho' not an absolute objection to taking them again : for I should think it your Interest as a Tradesman who wishes to recommend himself, to endeavour to oblige, and to prefer taking back a Thing which does not please to having it produced in the world, and censur'd as well as the Workman. If these Candlesticks were to be kept by me they would as often as produced be observed as very ugly & ill finished.'

Turning now to Sheffield, where most of the candlesticks of the Adam period were made, the situation is complicated by the proliferation of names which occur in the records. It is not possible to associate a particular design exclusively with one man, or even with one family, resulting in an almost mediaeval anonymity about this aspect of Sheffield production. It seems that plate-workers not only exchanged dies but to make matters more confused traded parts, if not whole objects, with one another. There is no point here in listing the various families and their numerous groupings and re-groupings as Bradbury in his classic work on Sheffield Plate[1] has already done so. Almost all objects, it should be emphasized, could be made in fused plate or silver. Suffice it to say then that the Sheffield men liked to market different kinds of wares under different combinations of names and that some of the best silver of the time may be linked, from its marks, with the following : Thomas Law, Henry Tudor and Thomas Leader, John Winter, Matthew Fenton and Richard Creswick, Richard Morton, George Ashforth, Samuel Roberts, Daniel Holy and Joseph Creswick. This is by no means an exclusive list. Law was rooted in the cutlery trade having served his apprenticeship in it, and in fact he became Master Cutler in 1753. Neither Tudor nor Leader were natives of Sheffield, but came to the town largely through the enterprise of a Dr. Sherburn who had the foresight to see, in the case of Leader, that a skilled London silversmith might help the growing industry. It is not clear what qualifications Tudor had, but he was prominent in the partnership and registered a mark at Goldsmiths' Hall prior to 1773. Bradbury says that theirs was the earliest 'factory' in connection with the plate industry and they appear to have made a fortune. John Winter, like Matthew Fenton, served his apprenticeship with Thomas Law. He was by far the biggest maker in the candlestick trade, and we learn from Sam Roberts junr., and can check from the Assay Office records at

[1] F. Bradbury : *History of Old Sheffield Plate*, Macmillan 1912.

Sheffield, that although he joined other partnerships making different things he continued to specialize in candlesticks with John Parsons, who in 1783 continued the business as John Parsons and Co. Later the firm went through many changes of name. In the 1780's and 1790's the partnership between Sam Roberts junr. and George Cadman was one of the most progressive and for innovations—which applied mainly to fused plate—among the few rivals of Boulton. (See pages 48–50.)

It follows that because of the rather peculiar conditions obtaining in Sheffield one has to think in terms of a Sheffield manner rather than the characteristic touch of any individual maker. With all the sources already discussed in mind we can look at the candlestick (Pl. 58) with a knowing eye. It is well balanced, bold, and the decoration interesting; it has even so a somewhat odd appearance, certainly from an academic point of view. This is hardly surprising when one realizes that the shaft derives from a classical tripod which has very simply been converted into a square form by the addition of another leg. If we look again at John Carter's candelabrum (Pl. 12), which appears highly sophisticated by contrast, that naive quality characteristic of Sheffield work at this time is emphasized. Motifs like rams' heads for instance were often treated with a careless abandon of their orthodox proportions and relationships to other elements. The results of this lack of respect for authority remind one of those charming thin metal candlesticks of the late seventeenth century which used a stumpy Doric column for a shaft.

Adamite motifs went on being used in Sheffield after the simple elegant forms of the last two decades of the century had become more fashionable. Some fine candlesticks too were made by adapting Flaxman designs (Pl. 62). One of the most popular patterns, to judge by the number still about, was a sort of clustered column affair with palm leaf capitals. The candlestick (Pl. 61A) was certainly made in Sheffield though it bears John Carter's initials and was marked in London (see p. 85). This pattern could be reduced in scale for tapersticks (Pl. 61B) or twisted to give variation (Pl. 60). The last produced a curious effect, but then the whole thing is an art historical nightmare; the proportion is more or less classical, the capital vaguely Egyptian, but the columns may refer to Salisbury cathedral or represent merely a bunch of bamboos.

Some of the very best Sheffield candlesticks were made in the 80's and 90's (Pl. 63). At this stage the Sheffield men really seem to have come of age for there is a quiet maturity about their work which was unsurpassed. They were probably the first to employ the oval shape for objects whose use did not suggest it; an oval soup-tureen for example was obvious enough, but not an oval candlestick. It is an interesting conjecture how much the simplicity and refinement—in the best sense of the term—was influenced by the new market opened up by Sheffield Plate. Did that sturdy middle class, which was now something to be catered for, really influence the taste of its betters or was it simply that the innate love of plainness and appreciation of the beauty of the metal unadorned had come full circle once more.

CHAPTER VI

London and the Second Phase
of Neo-Classicism

In the work of the London silversmiths we can see more clearly the stylistic changes which represent what one might call post-Adam neo-classicism—that epitomized by Henry Holland and James Wyatt, the latter already mentioned in connection with Matthew Boulton. There was always more variety in London-made silver, largely because mechanical methods were never applied to its production to anything like the same extent as they were in Birmingham and Sheffield and this meant that changes in fashion and indeed personal mannerisms could become manifest much more quickly. It was this individual touch—even Boulton could not compete with it—which ensured London's pre-eminence in the long run, especially after the initial shock of the technological revolution was spent.

There is a good case for saying that by about 1775 Robert Adam had made his contribution to architecture and the decorative arts. His most important work was done and the revolution in taste which will always be associated with his name had become an historical fact. Especially after this date the plagiarizers and camp followers were busy misunderstanding Adam's originality and emphasizing the more pedestrian aspects of his work *ad nauseam*. It was unfortunate too, if to be expected, that it was generally the clichés of the style which made up that Adam manner to be seen in European silver from Scandinavia to Southern Italy in the later 1770's. The inevitable reaction which became so violent and took such toll of Adam's work in the nineteenth century was beginning to show in avant-garde circles. Horace Walpole, that recording instrument so useful to art historians, was registering disapproval of Adam, in striking contrast to his earlier attitude. It is small wonder that descriptions such as 'Mr. Adam's gingerbread and sippets of embroidery' come readily to mind and in spite of being so often quoted remain trenchant. Walpole found Holland's work much to his taste; he liked its simplicity, but seems to have been shrewdly aware that there was little genius behind it. Holland, whose main work was the rebuilding of Carlton House, was sensible of the overall effect of his interiors and therefore designed furniture for them. It would be a mistake however to suggest that his work had any great influence; rather it was symptomatic of the move towards greater austerity, the cleaning up of the Adam style in a way which consciously and, it would appear, unconsciously brought English neo-classicism nearer to that of France. It is worth noting that Holland's chief assistant was a Frenchman.

The soup-tureen of 1780 by Thomas Heming (Pl. 64) provides an excellent illustration of what was afoot in fashionable quarters by this time. If we compare it with the Richmond race cup (Pl. 8) it seems in its measured simplicity to be deliberately anti-Adam and yet it belongs essentially to the eighteenth century, bearing little hint of the so-called Regency style to come. The decorative motifs are mainly textural, convex contrasted with concave fluting, reserved panels of matting and reeded bands. The acanthus leaves and palmettes are there, but used only with the utmost discretion. And this last is perhaps the key word for the whole piece. Thomas Heming became principal goldsmith to the crown in 1760. Major-General Sitwell[1] says that he was the first, since the civil war at any rate, to have a registered maker's mark of his own; this no doubt points to the changing status of the Royal Goldsmiths from that, virtually, of bankers to tradesmen, albeit of a rather exalted kind. Heming provided the regalia and plate for the coronation of George III and enjoyed the custom of the great. While his royal connection must have helped him he was a fine craftsman who knew his worth and charged accordingly; the standing cup (Pl. 23) does him much credit. He ceased to hold his appointment, which had never been by warrant, in 1782 the same year that the Jewel House was abolished. Possibly he was considered too expensive in the face of the Lord Chamberlain's investigations, or it may have been simply that a change was

---

[1] H. D. W. Sitwell: 'The Jewel House and the Royal Goldsmiths', *The Archaeological Journal*, Vol. CXVII.

thought desirable after over twenty years. Whatever the reason his successor certainly proved cheaper.

The massive tureen (Pl. 65) though made a dozen years later than Heming's has much in common with it, especially in the flattened fluting which in this case has become completely French and might be from the hand of Auguste himself. Wakelin and Garrard and their predecessors have already been considered, but in this piece and indeed in the much earlier baskets and stands (Pl. 66) the Parisian touch noticeable in a lot of the firm's work is very much in evidence. It can be seen also in the fine commemorative tureen[1] (Pl. 67) though rather less obviously. French influence, especially the massiveness associated with the transition from the Louis XV to the Louis XVI manner, is to be found a good deal earlier still in candlesticks and candelabra (Pls. 70, 71A and 71B). It was as if to the rich of the 1770's luxury and extravagance were symbolized by the French candlestick whether it were made in precious metal or in ormolu.

The Doncaster race cup (Pl. 68), another fine piece by Wakelin and Taylor it will be remembered, brings us firmly home again, for it is possessed of a very English elegance. It would surely not be too imaginative to see an affinity between this cup and the Darwin tureen[2] of 1790 (Pl. 69B) by Fogelberg and Gilbert. The tureen goes that much further towards minimal decoration and uses with subtle effect the beading, so characteristic a feature of the work of these makers, to pick up the pointed termination of the fluted areas. A sauce-tureen made a few years earlier (Pl. 75B) is enriched with a band of flowers and buds connected by curving tendrils which give a rhythmic swing to the design. If we compare this with two bands of decoration, one cast, the other chased, on the teapot made a year or two before (Pl. 73) it would appear that the familiar wave pattern provided the idea for all the variations. The teapot is in itself something of a

---

[1] The tureen is decorated with a canal scene in low relief on one side and on the other the inscription: 'The Company of the Proprietors of the Navigation from the Trent to the Mersey to Thomas Gilbert Esq., M.P., as a testimony of their Gratitude for his long and important services in parliament and on all other occasions to that undertaking.' Gilbert, remembered mainly for his poor law activities, backed James Brindley and did much to promote canal building.

[2] The tureen bears the arms of Robert Waring Darwin and his wife Susannah who was the daughter of Josiah Wedgwood. Robert was the son of Dr. Erasmus Darwin mentioned by Joseph Priestley (see p. 56) and father of Charles Darwin the naturalist.

curiosity, it is pretty enough to look at, but must have been a hazardous object to use. The ram's headed stand admittedly kept the heat from the table, but it asked a lot of a hostess, while carrying on a conversation, to concentrate enough on what she was doing to replace the teapot safely after pouring. Perhaps one aberration with a boat-shaped object full of hot tea would have been enough to fix its working principles in mind—or determine the owner to use it only for show in the future. To be fair, the bottom is slightly flattened which might conceivably have saved the day in an emergency landing. Strangely enough this design appears to have evolved from a teapot almost exactly similar in form but with an orthodox foot rim (Pl. 74).

A feature of some of the silver emanating from the workshop of these makers was the applied medallion (Pls. 75A, 76A and 76B). While other silversmiths occasionally decorated their work with medallions of classical themes or portraits, for example Smith and Sharp (Pl. 1), John Schofield (Pl. 94) and the maker of the sauce-tureen (Pl. 77), Mr. Oman has pointed out that Fogelberg and Gilbert, at least, relied directly on Tassie's vitreous-paste repro-ductions of gemstones as models. It is possible that they supplied the medallions for the jewel casket, mirror and boxes of the silver-gilt toilet service of 1779 in Stockholm[1]—another important commission executed by Smith and Sharp (Pl. 78). The medallion on the casket, the Marriage of Cupid and Psyche, was taken from a gem once in the Marlborough collection; this was certainly among the thousands reproduced by Tassie.

James Tassie was well known in his own day and his work much admired among the cognoscenti hence the facilities given him for taking moulds from engraved gemstones in collections all over Europe. As well as reproducing classical and renaissance gems he did original portrait work, practising the various aspects of his art just at the time when there was the greatest demand for it, and indeed he helped in his turn to encourage the appreciation of classical art. He used an easily fusable glass for making moulds from the originals as well as for taking impressions from the moulds; this was a great improvement on the methods of earlier medallists, fine detail was possible and the casts were not easily damaged. The first catalogue of Tassie's gemstone impressions

---

[1] See Arthur Grimwade: 'Royal Toilet Services in Scandinavia', *Connoisseur*, April 1956.

was published in 1775 and among the crowned heads who bought complete sets of his reproductions was Catherine of Russia who, incidentally, had hers sent out in cabinets specially designed by James Wyatt. Wedgwood was another of Tassie's customers, he was supplied with moulds for some of the portraits from which he made castings with his own paste. Today one of the best and most accessible collections of Tassie's work is to be found in the Scottish National Portrait Gallery.

Until he moved to what is now Leicester Square in 1778 Tassie's workshop was very near the premises occupied by Andrew Fogelberg in Church Street, and we may suspect that the two men knew each other well. Fogelberg appears to have established himself as a London silversmith, about 1770, and probably a few years later decided that, based on his neighbour's work, he could make silver casts of almost inexhaustible variety which might be applied to his own products. The effect was usually good, but in some cases, especially on the earlier examples, the medallions look like an after-thought squeezed in to add distinction (Pl. 75A). It is reasonable to assume that he soon went one step further and exported these silver 'Tassie' medallions to Sweden,[1] very likely the country of his own origin and training. Swedish neo-classical silver incorporating adaptations of Tassie's work is not rare; similar details appear in Danish work too. It should be remembered however that the idea of the small medallion as a decorative motif on silver was not new in Sweden and in fact goes back to the seventeenth century. In 1780 Fogelberg took Stephen Gilbert into partnership. Gilbert had served his apprenticeship with Edward Wakelin over twenty years before, so that he had had a good grounding in a first-class workshop; he subsequently worked on his own for a bit and may have been employed by Fogelberg prior to the partnership. Judging by the little we know of either silversmith and from the plate in existence made before 1780 and therefore bearing Fogelberg's mark only, one might suppose that he was the more imaginative partner responsible for most of the ideas. That his mind worked on unorthodox lines is borne out well by the early soup-tureen of 1770, possibly the year he entered his mark (Pl. 72), in which the festoons look as though they have been squeezed from a cornucopia. Certainly some of the

[1] See Charles Oman : 'Andrew Fogelberg and the English influence on Swedish Silver', *Apollo*, June 1947.

most original and interesting silver of the period came from the workshop in Church Street, Soho.[1] It was to Fogelberg that Paul Storr was apprenticed about 1785 and the latter's early work is very much in the tradition of his master. Dr. Penzer illustrates a teapot of 1799 bearing Storr's mark[2] which is the same basic design as that shown in Pl. 73, and the sauce-tureen (Pl. 75B) was repeated almost exactly by Storr in 1793.[3]

All the way through the history of English silversmithing the art of engraving—one of the most ancient and venerable methods of decoration—has ebbed and flowed, and during the neo-classical period it was on the ebb. The reasons are fairly obvious, for during the Adam boom of the late 1760's and 70's there was so much three-dimensional ornament that it was aesthetically essential, as we have seen, to leave any blank intervals unscarred. One has the feeling that the inclusion of a customer's arms was often resented by the craftsman, a case in point being the Kandler wine-cooler (Pl. 29) in which no place had been left for them. No skill seems so quickly to lose vitality when little practised as engraving, and the armorial work of our period, if often efficient enough, was usually pedestrian (Pl. 79A). The same sort of thing happened during the early seventeenth century when plain surfaces were so much admired and then it was over a hundred years before the engraving associated with Ellis Gamble and Hogarth rivalled in verve and quality that of the Elizabethans. As always exceptions come to mind as soon as one generalizes and the salver of 1770 (Pl. 79B) is one of them, for the engraving is certainly the most distinguished feature of it. The piece itself with its pretty curvilinear rim is reminiscent of Wright's coffee-pot (Pl. 18) in that it stands somewhere between the rococo and the neo-classical. It is as if the engraver had decided to make it quite clear however that he was all for the latter. There is a naive charm, a quality to be discerned in so much of the best English work of all ages, in what he has done (the armorials are almost certainly by a different hand and were no doubt added when the piece was sold); there are four different sorts of classical urn, all reasonably orthodox, and four animal masks performing their accepted tasks of holding

[1] For a summary of what is known about Fogelberg and Gilbert see N. M. Penzer: *Paul Storr*, B. T. Batsford, 1954, pp. 51–57.
[2] N. M. Penzer: op. cit., Pl. IV.
[3] N. M. Penzer: op. cit., Pl. VII.

up the swags, rather less orthodox and full of humour. Indeed the quality of this work in both concept and execution has something Hogarthian about it.

A new form of engraving became very popular in the 1780's known as 'bright-cutting'. This was so executed that hundreds of little facets were created, at an angle to the surface of the piece, which caught the light and produced a mildly glittering effect. It must have been dreadfully tedious to do and could be very mechanical in appearance. It is difficult to appreciate its effect today, however, except on the occasional piece still in mint condition because ordinary wear and tear soon destroyed its sharpness. Plates 81, 82 and 90 show good examples of this work.

It is tempting to see a feminine touch in what one might call the two-dimensional taste of the last decades of the eighteenth century. But perhaps the wish is prompted by the knowledge that some women artists were held in particularly high regard then. Two of them, Mary Moser, the painter of those charming if somewhat vapid flower pieces, and Angelica Kauffmann with her 'sweet' portraits and classical pastiches—they usually included children— were made foundation members of the Royal Academy, a great honour indeed. Robert Adam found the latter's work an excellent foil to Zucchi's architectural capricci and he gave extensive commissions to both of them. Although the two painters married and left England in 1781, Angelica's influence especially was strongly established by this time.

By far the most famous of the women silversmiths of these years, and there were a number of them, was Hester Bateman.[1] If cynically inclined it would perhaps be not unfair to attribute some of her renown in America at least to that country's matriarchal tendencies. Be that as it may, by any standards she was a remarkable woman with a remarkable family. From Bunhill Row for nearly thirty years they produced silverware under Hester's mark, first registered in 1761. It was she who built up the business from scratch and when during the 1780's it was thoroughly established, with a reputation for high quality work, Hester had with her sons and grandsons as well as her daughter-in-law Ann. After Hester's retirement in 1790 Peter and Jonathan registered their mark, but in a matter of months the latter died and the firm was known under the mark of Peter and Ann until after our period. Characteristic of

[1] See David S. Shure : *Hester Bateman*, W. H. Allen, 1959.

this family business was the consistency of its aims. It produced useful wares, teapots, cream-jugs, salts, and a variety of other things that would appeal particularly to the middle classes, and especially to those of them who were well enough off to buy silver for their tables rather than Sheffield plate. There were of course special commissions, but they do not contribute to the Bateman image today, and almost certainly did not then. The teapot and stand (Pl. 82) and the cruet (Pl. 90) are typical pieces with their oval shape, beaded edges and bright-cut engraving which was a speciality of the workshop. The Batemans must have been very proud of the tea-urn (Pl. 81). This, from its supremely elegant form and beautiful handles to the quality of its chasing and engraving, is indeed a masterpiece.

The very slightness of current ornament, as well as its two-dimensional characteristics, served to emphasize shape and pro-portion (Pls. 83 and 85). A great deal of care was taken over these and sometimes superb effects obtained by juxtaposing the simplest geometric forms. A good example is the water-jug (Pl. 89) by Thomas Daniel in which the facetted pineapple with its spikey leaves is cunningly used as a foil to the undecorated surfaces below. Polygonal designs were used frequently (Pls. 84A, 84B, 88 and 89); they were a logical step once silversmiths again thought in terms of plain reflecting surfaces. Perhaps the word plain is ambiguous when applied to silver for the polished metal creates abstract patterns from its environment according to the curves and straights put upon it. The Huguenot refugees had been adept at exploiting these qualities and they used polygonal forms to superb effect too. And yet, with all the obvious similarities in the appreciation of the material as such, there is a world of difference between the products of the early and the late eighteenth century. Today current aesthetic standards lead us to rank both very highly; we look upon the Huguenot period as archaic, neverthe-less, and value it partly for this reason, while the silver we have been thinking about in the last few pages often seems strikingly modern. What a delightful object the teapot is (Pl. 83) and only on second thoughts are we likely to be aware that it is nearly two hundred years old.

A master of reflections was John Schofield, another silversmith, like John Carter and Daniel Smith and Robert Sharp, sometime of Bartholomew Close. In the magnificent cruets, one of his two specialities—the other being candelabra—he used the glass bottles standing on plain polished plateaux (Pls. 91ʙ and 92) in very much the same manner as wall mirrors were contrived to make play with the lights and colours in glass chandeliers. While a typical Schofield candelabrum sums up what has been said about post-Adam neo-classicism—its supreme elegance, proportion and balance (Pls. 94 and 95ᴀ)—a closer analysis of his decorative repertoire is instructive and can best be seen in the cruets and other of his more massive plate. He obviously had another good look at the neo-classical source material discussed in earlier chapters, for instance the palm leaf motif which he used so often (Pls. 91ʙ and 93) was very likely suggested by an illustration in d'Hancarville's *Vases* (Pl. 91ᴀ). Taking into consideration that he was a consummate craftsman there is nevertheless a new crispness and three-dimensionality in his work which is a matter of conception rather than of execution. This can be seen very well in the feet and in the handles and lids of the bottles on the cruet (Pl. 91ʙ). All this, coupled with a flowery flowing naturalism, looks forward to the solidity and technical mastery of Paul Storr and his peers.

There are no hard and fast divisions between styles any more than there are between reigns when it comes to economic history, but with Schofield, deeply rooted in the eighteenth century while tentatively poking a toe into the future, one might reasonably end a stylistic survey of English neo-classical silver before the Regency.

CHAPTER VII

Marketing, Competition and Prices

During the last quarter of the eighteenth century a greater variety of things was made in silver than at any previous time, most of them self-explanatory and it would therefore be tedious to list them. It might be useful, however, to comment on some of the objects which appear in the catalogues of the day under ambiguous or new names. The tea-urn—sometimes referred to as a 'kitchen'—came into use in the early 1760's, superseding the tea-kettle, and had its heyday during the neo-classical period. The water was kept hot by inserting a heated iron into the inner liner; the whole vessel stood on a base usually with four feet and it had a tap on the front. Unlike the teapot it proved a particularly suitable object for vase treatment and the tap could be made an object of decoration adding to the elegance of the whole (Pl. 81). The elaborate apparatus consisting of tea, coffee and water containers and sometimes a slop-basin, often called, no doubt for want of a better description, a 'machine', belongs more to the early years of the nineteenth century. These illustrate, however, the vogue for furniture and fittings which performed more than one task—the dressing-table-cum-writing-desks or the harlequin tables incorporating work-boxes—the sort of things that appear among Thomas Sheraton's designs. In the field of silver many of the gadgets and patterns which improved the efficiency of everyday objects emanated from Birmingham or Sheffield. The greatest ingenuity was concentrated upon lighting appliances—from folding and telescopic candlesticks to Argand's lamp. The story of the last is a sad one, for the inventor, a Swiss physician called Aimé Argand, saw his patent revoked on a point of law and himself deprived of most of the profits of his brain-child. The lamp was in fact one of the outstanding inventions of the century and had the simplicity of genius about it—this was Argand's undoing, because it could so easily be copied once the idea was out of the bag. Before the days of the self-consuming candle-wick it would be an understatement to say that lighting was smelly and smoky; both candles and lamps suffered from similar defects. The principle of Argand's lamp was that of a thin tubular wick in a glass chimney; this meant that the air reached both sides of the wick and an upward draft was ensured. Argand came to England in 1783 and soon got in touch with Boulton who was to make most of the parts of the lamp; a few were to be made in London, the wicks in Manchester. If the patent of 1784 had been upheld both Boulton and the inventor would have done well. There is a most interesting correspondence in the Assay Office at Birmingham, including a specification for the lamp, in which is discussed improvements that might be made. The problem of getting a suitable fuel exercised their minds; olive oil seems to have given good results, but presumably was expensive, and attempts were made to purify spermaceti oil. In the event Boulton was only one of many makers, but demand was high and he produced a number of different designs at Soho in silver, Sheffield plate, ormolu and glass. In the same generic category as lighting appliances come tapersticks and their variations; though their flames were intended primarily for sealing letters they had a use as easily portable lights. During our period there were many patterns on the market, usually called either taper-winders or wax-jacks, but the name bougie box appears in a number of catalogues; this was the small drum type about three inches in diameter with a funnel at the top through which the wax taper, curled up inside, could protrude (Pl. 87A). The bodies were sometimes plain, at others pierced, and were almost certainly shared with mustard pots—the popular glass-lined sort. They simply had a modified top and provision for an extinguisher. Most of them quite cheap, they provide another example of the uninhibited practice, already noticed, of making the most of a useful design.

During the neo-classical period catalogues were issued by an increasing number of Sheffield plate firms. They seem to have been printed primarily for retailers to show customers, and from the surviving fragments one can get a good idea of the range of everyday objects marketed, as well as of the most popular patterns. Makers' names were not included, a pity for posterity, but occasionally clues to identity are found such as initials: TL for

instance which presumably refers to Tudor and Leader. No doubt the very considerable expense of printing was worth it, as most of the goods, being quantity produced and cheap, could in fact be ordered by this means. These catalogues are relevant to the history of silver in so far as the more precious material might be looked upon as an alternative to fused plate.

Of a different order are the books of patterns from Soho now in the Birmingham Reference Library.[1] These represent part at least of the working material from the design department of one of the leading firms making neo-classical silver, and their importance is therefore far wider than their Birmingham context at first suggests. The most interesting part of the hoard consists of drawings, from thumb-nail sketches to finished designs, covering a period from about 1760 to the 1840's. A number of existing pieces may be linked with the patterns which, incidentally, present a somewhat odd appearance today, because they have been tidied up and stuck in order of subject on the pages of several large volumes; unfortunately in the process some were cut so close that pattern numbers and notes may have been lost. Many of the large-scale working drawings (Pls. 40, 48, 49, 53 and 55B) are beautifully rendered and detailed; three of those illustrated may be compared with the objects produced from them (Pls. 41, 52 and 54). No finished drawings exist now for the water-jug (Pl. 45) or the sauce-tureen (Pl. 56A) but the little sketches from which they would have been evolved can be identified, the latter for example may be found among the sauce-tureens (Pl. 57). This sheet of patterns is particularly interesting in showing a few of the excellent variations Soho could produce on the two themes of upswept or ring handles. Another group of sketches, this time of soup-tureens (Pl. 47), is worthy of attention for all five are clearly designs for special commissions and from two of them the fine drawings already referred to (Pls. 48 and 49) have been worked up. The middle one, for which unfortunately there is no more detailed drawing preserved, is inscribed 'Soup Tureen made for the Admiralty 1781' and was the subject of a considerable and highly informative correspondence. It was a repeat order for a tureen made some ten years before on which the following paragraphs, in a letter sent from Soho on October 5th 1771, throw

---

[1] See W. A. Seaby and R. S. Hetherington: 'The Matthew Boulton Pattern Books', *Apollo*, February and March 1950.

light. To 'James Stuart Esq, Agreeable to the Contents of your much Esteemed Letter of 28th of last month we have forwarded the Silver Terrine in a Box marked W M No. 326 pr Wagon, Carriage note directed to Philip Stephens Esqr at the Admiralty, we hope it will please and as you mention that the Engraving was to be done in London we have omitted it.

Sorry we are that the Value of this piece surpasses so far the sum of £100 = you fixed on for it, but from our inexperience in the making of such large pieces of work, (it weighed 341 ozs.) and having some doubts if you did not mean £100 intrinsick Value, besides having made it larger than we Intended—by the mistake of a workman—We have we fear exseedded the sum the Admiralty intended, and therefore as it is our Mistake from inexperience, we submit ourselves to th^r honour, which we believe no man ever complain'd off'. Across the letter in red ink is written 'The Invoice of the Terrine for the Lords Commissioners of the Admiralty Amounting to £140.16/- went inclosed in this letter'. Fothergill thought that the second tureen, that of 1781, was a highly desirable commission and on the 2nd of April that year John Hodges wrote to Boulton, who was away from home, saying 'By desire of Mr. Fothergill I have now to inform you that the Silver Terrene & Dish wanted for the Admiralty can with readiness be executed at Soho.

Some of the old Sketches as well as models (for the previous one) are found and upon consulting with Mr. Bingley we find there is no doubt but that it can be well executed by the hands employ'd here—Mr. Willson & Mr. Hooker can do the chasing part . . .'. On April 4th he wrote again saying 'By Monday's post I had the pleasure of writing to you—Herewith is a drawing of the Terrene same as made for the Admiralty in 1771—annex'd is an estimate of the expense which is as near as can be ascertained and Mr. Bingley thinks it cannot be well got up for less—we think it should not be undertaken for less than 5/- per oz or at least 4/6 per oz but as you have the cost you can undertake it as you may judge fit—One of the workmen who assisted in making the last is now at Soho & who has been consulted about the making, expense etc—I have to observe that that before made for the Admiralty was charged no more than 2/6 per oz fashion . . . which 'tis presumed must be considerably under *prime* cost, especially when the expense of modelling is taken in—On enquiry of the Silversmiths here they suppose that the Londoners would not execute it for less than 5/– pr oz but of this you can be easily satisfied—This drawing I expected to send last night according to my promise, but Mr. Wilson (one of the chasers mentioned in the previous letter) could not finish it in time and even now he has not finished it near so well as he could have done had he had more time etc.'. This letter is worth quoting *in extenso* for it not only provides information about charges for fashion of the highest quality work in London but gives further hints of the difficulties the provincial maker had in wresting an important commission from London in 1771 before Soho's reputation was fully established or the Birmingham Assay Office in existence. In the end Boulton decided to calculate on 4s. 6d. per ounce fashion for the second tureen. For the first he seems to have had to reduce his charges below cost, but the figure of 2s. 6d. per ounce fashion given by Hodges is likely to have been worked out to minimize the result of exceeding the terms of the order, or from the price eventually agreed by the Admiralty, rather than be a figure calculated to compete with London. In 1771 Boulton was certainly at the Commissioners' mercy. In passing it may be noted that for less exalted work Soho seems to have charged something under 2s. per ounce fashion— fairly simple candlesticks perhaps on which, incidentally, round bases cost less than square—to about 3s. 3d. or so. Silver itself of course varied in price according to the state of the market, but around 1779 to 1780 a probable average cost would have been 5s. 6d. to 5s. 9d. per ounce. It is therefore possible, provided one knows the weight of a piece, to work out its likely retail price. Another thing that comes out in this correspondence is the impor- tance of the chaser and how responsible he was for the aesthetic merit of the finished object. The reputation of a firm virtually depended upon the quality of the chasers it employed, and it was highly desirable to keep their hands in, a point clearly made in a further letter from Hodges on the same subject dated April 9th 1781. 'My last to you was the 4th ins' accompanying a drawing of a Dolphin Terrene etc. respecting which have further to observe that if the order is undertaken it will give some employ to the Silversmiths and Chasers who are now neither much busied.' By the end of November the Lords of the Admiralty were annoyed that the tureen had not been delivered and were only prevented from writing a nasty letter demanding an explanation by the good offices of Boulton's friend, Sir Joseph Banks, who was present at the meeting. Great efforts appear to have been made at Soho with the result that a letter could be written to James Stuart on December 29th containing the following passage: 'Sir, We have the pleasure to inform you that the Terrene is at length finished and forwarded per wagon addressed to Philip Stephens Esqʳ at Whitehall—It has been longer in hand than we expected, yet we assure you we have been *as expeditious as possible* therewith, taking care that no pains or expense should be wanting to make it as highly finished as in our power; and we have the satisfaction to say that we do not doubt but that it will meet the honour of the *Admiralty's approbation.*' Stuart ordered the tureens and may very well have been responsible for at least the basic design too.

On the subject of marketing we know that most of the larger London firms acted as retailers and sold the work of other silver-smiths as well as their own products. To take one example, Wakelin and Taylor had a long list of silversmiths from whom they bought all sorts of everyday wares. These included candle-sticks from John Carter, who as we shall see himself bought quantities of candlesticks from Sheffield, and various items from Matthew Boulton. The latter's accounts show that he supplied them with such things as ice-pails, candlesticks and sugar-basins in ormolu, silver and plate, and that he gave them the usual trade discount of 20 per cent plus 5 per cent for prompt payment! This is over and above the purchase of machine made parts for simple objects like cream-jugs which Sheffield and Birmingham firms had been supplying for decades. These parts could be had for about half what they would have cost to make by the comparatively laborious traditional methods. The Sheffield men worked much for the trade and in 1773 formed themselves into an association mainly with the idea it seems of fixing minimum prices, permissible discounts and that sort of thing. Member firms who did not send representatives to meetings were fined 2s. 6d. The minutes of the meetings tell one little except that there was really not much that could be done against offenders; when someone did under-sell or over-charge decisions on what action should be taken were nearly always deferred to a future meeting. The association ceased to function in 1784.

Particularly before the establishment of its own assay office it would have been easy to pass off Sheffield silver as London made. It was in any case nearly always hall-marked in London. Apart from that which bore the registered mark of the real maker, a large part of the output of, for example, John Winter's candlestick firm was set aside for the trade. It would therefore have had London maker's marks as well as hall-marks and been sold very profitably by the middle man at London prices. Many vested interests conflicted with the establishment of the Birmingham and Sheffield assay offices and after they were successfully set up one would not have to look very far for a motive behind the London overmarking of silver already fully marked in Sheffield. This appears to have been a not uncommon practice, with candlesticks especially, mainly between about 1775 and 1780.[1] In many examples still in existence it is not all that hard to decipher the Sheffield crown beneath the leopard's head of London. The most frequently found overstruck maker's mark is that of John Carter whose work was discussed in Chapter III—this may be because candlesticks formed the bulk of his business—but there were other men such as John Schofield, who indulged in this practice. No doubt Goldsmiths' Hall were only too willing to re-assay upstart provincial plate in the hopes of finding something below standard, and if they were disappointed in this, as they always were, by the same process they could claim for their London fraternity a worthy piece of silver. There were in fact comparatively few London-made neo-classical candlesticks on the market after about 1775.

Matthew Boulton, in common with many of his London rivals, relied mainly on his patrons and personal recommendation for his more important commissions. As might be expected from a man who had opinions on almost every subject, his views on marketing are worth some attention. He took a poor view of common shop-keepers, calling them the 'Bane of all improvements', a view shared incidentally by James Adam, and did not like the idea of them reaping undeserved profits. This no doubt is one of the reasons why from time to time he sold his stocks of 'Fine Wares', those made without commissions, by auction at Messrs. Christie and Ansell's.[2] A sale in April 1771, for which a catalogue is preserved,

---

[1] See S. W. Turner: 'The Establishment and Development of the Silver and Plate Industry in Sheffield', *Apollo*, December 1947. And for examples of overmarked plate at Trinity College and St. John's College Cambridge, E. A. Jones: 'Two problems in the Hall-Marking of Silver', *Burlington Magazine*, June 1935.

[2] See Seaby and Hetherington: op. cit.; and E. Robinson: 'Eighteenth-Century Commerce and Fashion: Matthew Boulton's Marketing Techniques', *The Economic History Review*, Vol. XVI, No. 1, 1963.

consisted almost entirely of ormolu; another, seven years later, was more comprehensive. If these were typical, then this method of disposing of stock must have been disappointing, for though most of the lots were sold they often, especially in the second sale, did not reach their reserves. The thing that really mattered was the advertisement value of these sales; they were fashionable occasions and certainly in Boulton's case led to future orders from the nobility and gentry. It should be added that avoiding the middle-man in this way was not original to Boulton; there was a sale, for example, in the same rooms—also in April 1771—of Chelsea-Derby porcelain on behalf of Messrs. Dewsbury and Co.

As we have seen in Chapter V, Boulton corresponded with James Adam over the possibility of having premises in the Adelphi. In one of his letters Boulton described what he thought would make an ideal show-room. This was to be an elegant upstairs apartment having the advantage of being safe from 'Street walking pirates'; it would attract, he thought, the right sort of customers who preferred a little privacy. He went on to point out that all the best shops in Paris were upstairs. The suggestion caught Adam's fancy and he replied 'Your Idea also of the warehouse in preferment to the shop, is what I have been turning much in my mind, since I received Yours, & upon my word the longer I think of it, I like it the better. The novelty alone of such a thing would attract all ranks in this great Capital, where novelty and fashion carry every-thing irresistably before them. Your Idea therefore of such a warehouse lighted from the top, by a sky light pleas'd me greatly & the more so, as I know from experience, that every object whatever shows to more advantage in that light than in any other'.[1]

The most important step forward in marketing his silverware, and indeed that of Sheffield in its own right, was Boulton's successful campaign for the setting up of the new assay offices. The story has been told in full elsewhere,[2] but the salient features must be recounted here for they have very much more than local significance. The silversmiths of both towns were under great hardship in having to send their plate so far afield to be hall-marked. It was not so much a matter of distance as of transport facilities; in

[1] James Adam to Matthew Boulton, 5 November 1770.
[2] See Arthur Westwood: *The Assay Office at Birmingham*, Part I.

practice most Birmingham silver was sent to London, though some of it, Boulton's for example (see p. 63), went to Chester; Sheffield silver seems invariably to have gone to London. This was a time-consuming and expensive business at best. Objects might be well enough packed by the makers to withstand the outward journey, but there was no guarantee that they would be as carefully prepared for return. There were indeed a number of occasions on which consignments of plate arrived back at Soho in a ruined condition. Then there were the hazards of the open assay offices where any rival could see what was going through. Under the leadership of Boulton Birmingham and Sheffield decided to fight their battles together and both towns petitioned Parliament within a day of each other. Two special committees of the House of Commons were set up to deal with the petitions and counter-petitions, for there was considerable opposition from the Londoners as was to be expected. On the face of it the main objections they put forward were that the standard of wrought plate would not be safe; that as the two towns were non-corporate, and neither had a guild of goldsmiths, there was no body before whom an assay master could be sworn, and that fused plate was really imitation silver and a good guide to the real intentions of the petitioners. Among the many London silversmiths who gave evidence before the committees were John Carter, George Cowles, John Wakelin, Charles Wright, and David Hennell, some as we have seen having an obvious axe to grind. Boulton circulated two papers which set out very ably the main points of his case, this may be summarized as follows: 1. That London-made plate had no special value in workmanship or design. He struck a patriotic note by adding in feigned disgust that it owed much to foreign artists. 2. That the makers had an unfair advantage over their provincial fellows. 3. That their prices were exorbitant, which meant that in spite of the prevailing taste for plate only comparatively few rich people could afford it. 4. That the new assay offices—having to make their way—would be very particular over standards of purity. In the second of the papers he accuses London—and this was his trump-card—of marking sub-standard plate. This had to be proved or disproved, and one of the committees ordered that 22 pieces of London-made plate should be bought at 'public shops' and assayed by the King's assay master at the mint and by the head assayer at Goldsmiths' Hall; both reported that all but one piece were considerably below standard. This forerunner of the method employed by modern consumer protection exposed the practice of making wrought plate of inferior quality silver supplied by the refiners as 'Old Sterling' as opposed to 'Upright Sterling' which was of the legal standard. All this took place in the early months of 1773. By the end of May, with the help of Sir George Savile in the Commons and Lord Dartmouth in the Lords, the Assay Bill became law, and Matthew Boulton returned home in triumph to the sound of the bells being rung for him at Handsworth church.

The marks chosen for the new assay offices, a crown for Sheffield and an anchor for Birmingham, were possibly suggested by the fact that a lot of the business in connection with the Bill was done at the Crown and Anchor Tavern in the Strand. This otherwise unexceptional circumstance may therefore have had the amusing effect of causing an essentially inland town on no important river to be represented by an anchor.

The 70's and 80's proved to be the vintage years of Birmingham and Sheffield silver. As we have seen, Birmingham's reputation was so much in the hands of one man that it was the rise and gradual decline of Soho that mattered. In Sheffield the situation was less sensitive : in terms of weight of wrought silver assayed the peak years were 1776 and 1777, some eight years or so before the duty imposed on silver chattels favoured fused plate. The figures of nearly 49,700 ounces and 45,250 ounces respectively were not rivalled until the turn of the century—which takes us beyond the terms of this book.

Short Bibliography

Charles James Jackson: *An Illustrated History of English Plate Ecclesiastical and Secular*, 2 vols., Country Life and Batsford, 1911.

Charles Oman: *English Domestic Silver*, 3rd edition, A. and C. Black, 1949.

Gerald Taylor: *Silver. An Illustrated Introduction to British Plate from the Middle Ages to the Present Day*, Penguin Books, 1956.

Walter S. Prideaux: *Memorials of the Goldsmiths' Company*, 1335–1815, 2 vols., 1896–7.

Frederick Bradbury: *History of Old Sheffield Plate*, Macmillan, 1912.

Arthur T. Bolton: *The Architecture of Robert and James Adam*, 1758–1794, 2 vols., Country Life, 1922.

John Fleming: *Robert Adam and His Circle in Edinburgh and Rome*, John Murray, 1962.

Eileen Harris: *The Furniture of Robert Adam*, Alec Tiranti, 1963.

H. W. Dickinson: *Matthew Boulton*, Cambridge, 1937.

David S. Shure: *Hester Bateman*, W. H. Allen, 1959.

Index

1. *Soup tureen, gilt, one of a pair.*
Daniel Smith and Robert Sharp, 1776.
Messrs. Lumley.

Pl. XXIV

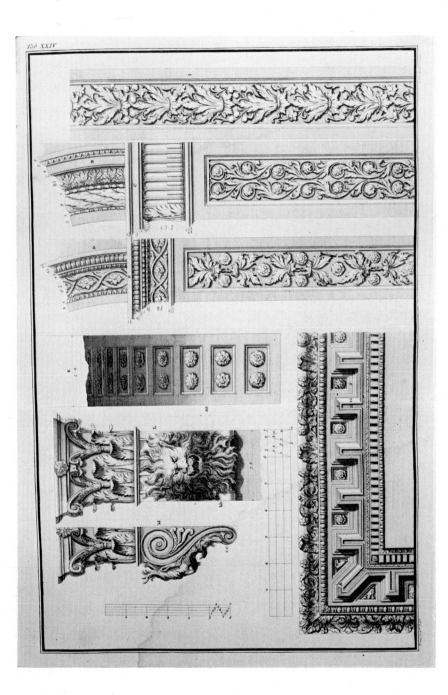

2. *Wood and Dawkins: 'Palmyra' 1753, Plate XXIV. Print Room and Art Library, Leeds.*

3. *d'Hancarville: William Hamilton's Collection, 1766–7,*
Vol. I, Plate 74. British Museum.

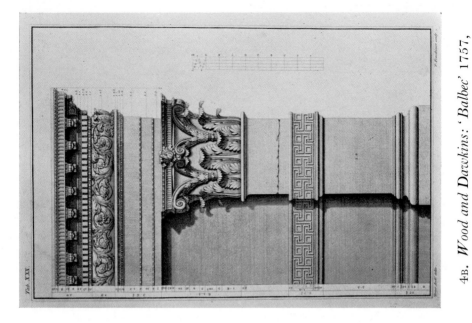

4B. *Wood and Dawkins: 'Balbec' 1757,*
Plate XXX. Print Room and Art

4A. *Wood and Dawkins: 'Balbec' 1757,*
Plate XX. Print Room and Art

Tab. XIX .

5. *Wood and Dawkins: 'Palmyra' 1753, Plate XIX.*
Print Room and Art Library, Leeds.

6. *Robert Adam: Drawing inscribed*
'Vase for Thomas Dundass Esqr for a Prize'.
Sir John Soane's Museum.

7. *Robert Adam: Drawing inscribed
'Vase for Thomas Dundas Esqr for a Prize'.
Sir John Soane's Museum.*

8. *The Richmond Race Cup, gilt.*
Daniel Smith and Robert Sharp, 1770.
Marquess of Zetland. H. 14½ in.

9. *The Richmond Race Cup (detail).*

10. *Candlestick, one of a pair. John Carter, 1767.*
Temple Newsam House, Leeds. H. 13⅝ *in.*

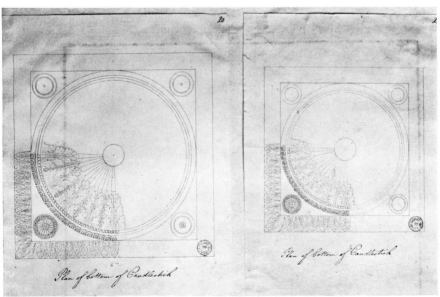

11A. *Adam Drawing, inscribed 'Design of a Candlestick'.*
Sir John Soane's Museum.
11B. *Two Adam Drawings, both inscribed*
'Plan of bottom of Candlestick'. Sir John Soane's Museum.

12. *Candelabrum, one of a set of four.*
John Carter, 1774.
Lloyd's of London. H. $14\frac{3}{4}$ *in.*

13. *Robert Adam: Drawing inscribed*
'*Candlestick for Sir Watkin Wynn Bart Adelphi 9th March 1773*'.
Sir John Soane's Museum.

14. *Soup tureen, gilt, one of a pair.*
James Young, 1778. Messrs. Lumley.

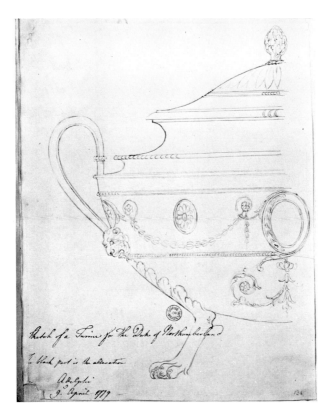

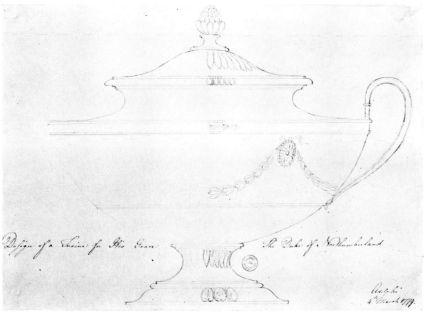

15A. *Adam Drawing, inscribed 'Sketch of a Turine
for The Duke of Northumberland Adelphi* 9th *April* 1779'.
Sir John Soane's Museum.
15B. *Adam Drawing, inscribed
'Design of a Turine for His Grace The Duke of Northumberland
Adelphi* 4th *March* 1779'. *Sir John Soane's Museum.*

16. *Soup tureen, gilt, one of a pair. James Young, 1778. Messrs. Lumley.*

17. *Soup tureen. Sebastian and James Crespell, 1771. Christie's. Diam. 12¼ in.*

18. *Coffee-pot. Charles Wright, 1776.*
Victoria and Albert Museum. H. 13½ *in.*

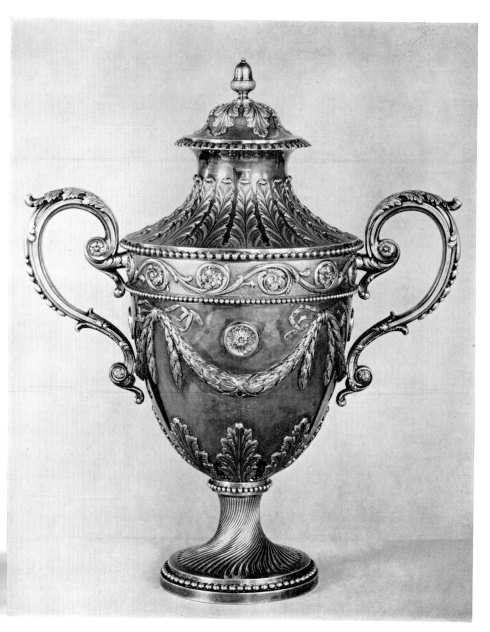

19. *Cup and cover. Louisa Courtauld and George Cowles, 1771.*
Victoria and Albert Museum. H. $14\frac{5}{8}$ *in.*

20. *The Greenaway Cup (finial later).*
William Holmes and Nicholas Dumée, 1774.
The Drapers' Company. H. 14½ in.

21. *Cup, cover and stand. William Holmes and Nicholas Dumée, 1774.*
Leeds Art Collections Fund. H. 21¾ *in.*

22A. *Cup and cover, gilt.*
William Holmes, 1775.
Walker Art Gallery,
Liverpool.
H. 15 in.

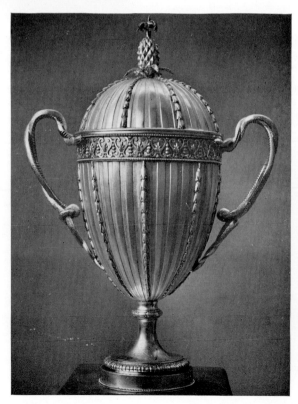

22B. *Cup and cover, gilt.*
William Holmes, 1776.
Walker Art Gallery,
Liverpool.
H. 18¾ in.

23. *Cup and cover, gilt. Thomas Heming, 1771.*
Trinity Hall, Cambridge. H. 11¾ in.

24A. *Tea-urn.*
Nicholas Dumée, 1776.
Christie's. H. 19¾ in.

24B. *Jug.*
Nicholas Dumée, 1777.
Messrs. Lumley.

25. *Chocolate-pot. Henry Greenway, 1777.*
Victoria and Albert Museum. H. $12\frac{1}{2}$ *in.*

26. *Tea-caddy. Louisa Courtauld and George Cowles, 1773.*
Victoria and Albert Museum. H. 3½ in.

27A. *Tea-caddy, gilt. Pierre Gillois, 1768.*
Victoria and Albert Museum. H. 5 in.
27B. *Tea-caddy, gilt. Augustin Le Sage, 1777.*
Victoria and Albert Museum. H. 4½ in.

28. *Salver, gilt, one of a pair. Frederick Kandler, 1775.*
Museum and Art Gallery, Birmingham. Diam. $14\frac{1}{2}$ in.

29. *Wine-cooler. Frederick Kandler, 1775.*
Victoria and Albert Museum. H. $7\frac{1}{2}$ *in.*

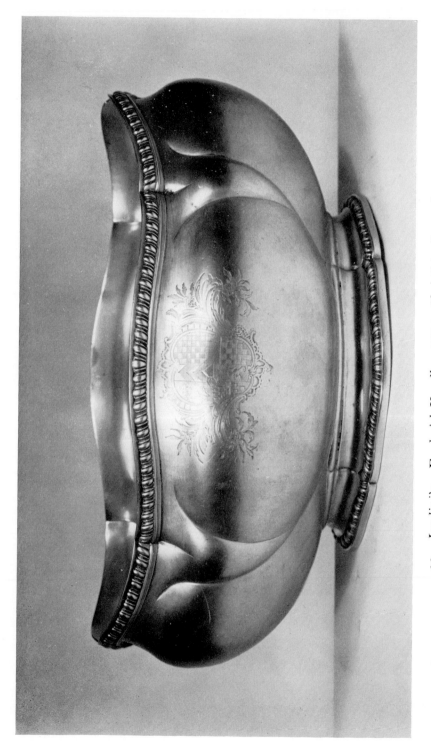

30. *Jardinière. Frederick Kandler, 1771. Christie's. L. 11 in.*

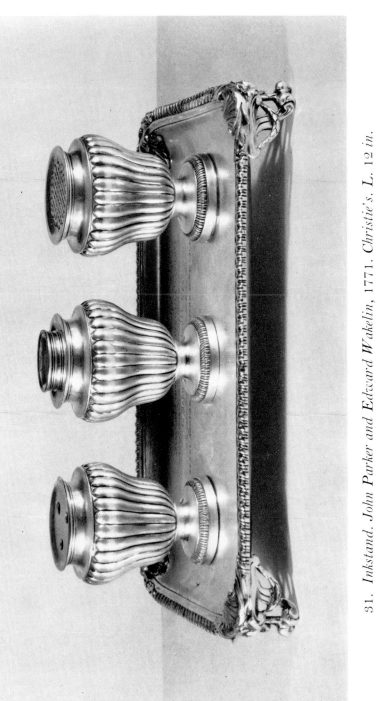

31. *Inkstand. John Parker and Edward Wakelin, 1771. Christie's. L. 12 in.*

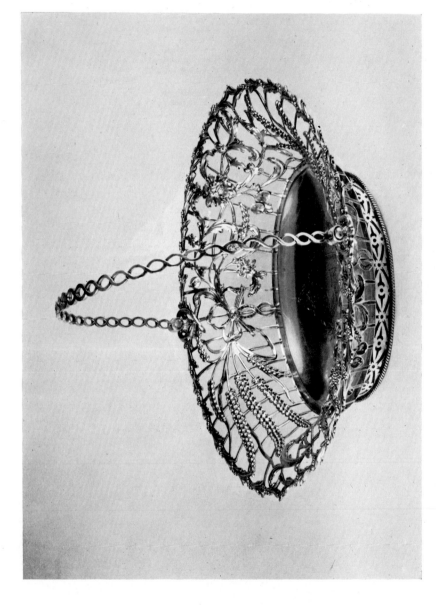

32. *Cake basket. Richard Mills, 1771. Victoria and Albert Museum. L. 13⅞ in.*

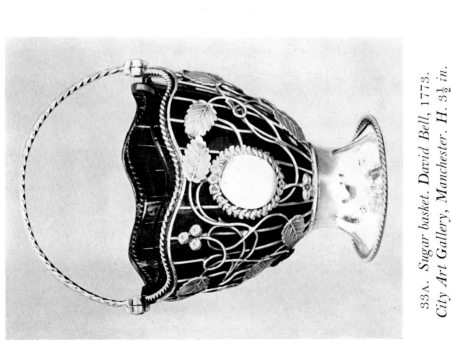

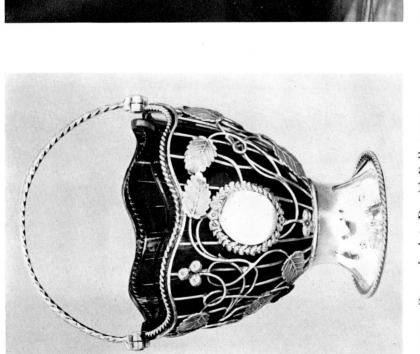

33B. *Cake basket. Matthew Boulton, Birmingham 1788.
Birmingham Assay Office. L. 12¼ in.*

33A. *Sugar basket. David Bell, 1773.
City Art Gallery, Manchester. H. 3½ in.*

34. *Cake basket. John Younge & Co., Sheffield* 1779.
Royal Academy, London. L. 12¾ *in.*

35A. *Cake basket. Burrage Davenport, 1777.*
Christie's. L. $13\frac{1}{2}$ in.
35B. *Cake basket. Charles Aldridge and Henry Green, 1783.*
Ashmolean Museum. L. $17\frac{1}{2}$ in.

36. *Epergne. Thomas Pitts, 1778.*
Victoria and Albert Museum. L. 30¼ in.

37A. *Epergne. John Wakelin and William Taylor, 1782. Messrs. Lumley.*
37B. *Epergne, gilt. Thomas Pitts, 1777. Messrs. Phillips.*

38. Soup tureen. John Parker and Edward Wakelin, 1775.
Messrs. Lumley.

39. *Soup tureen. John Wakelin and William Taylor*, 1778.
Pembroke College, Cambridge. H. $14\frac{1}{4}$ *in.*

40. *Boulton and Fothergill: Pattern for a jug.*
Birmingham Reference Library.

41. *Jug. Boulton and Fothergill, Birmingham* 1775.
Messrs. Lumley.

42. *Jug, parcel gilt. Boulton and Fothergill, Birmingham* 1776.
Courtesy, Museum of Fine Arts, Boston. H. 13½ *in.*

43. *d'Hancarville: William Hamilton's Collection, 1766–7. Vol. I, Plate 55.
British Museum.*

44. *d'Hancarville: William Hamilton's Collection, 1766–7.
Vol. II, Plate 23. British Museum.*

45. *Jug. Boulton and Fothergill, Birmingham* 1774.
Museum and Art Gallery, Birmingham. H. 13¾ *in.*

46. *M. A. Pergolesi: Designs for tureens. Published* 1782.
Birmingham Reference Library.

47. *Boulton and Fothergill: Patterns for tureens.*
Birmingham Reference Library.

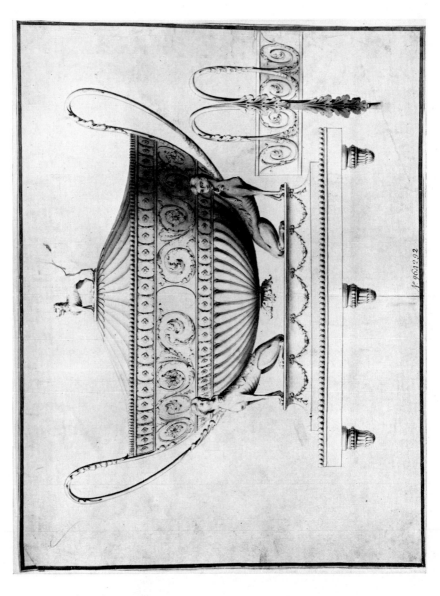

48. *Boulton and Fothergill: Pattern for a tureen. Birmingham Reference Library.*

49. *Boulton and Fothergill: Pattern for a tureen. Birmingham Reference Library.*

50. *Candlestick, one of a set of four.*
Boulton and Fothergill, Birmingham 1774.
Courtesy, Museum of Fine Arts, Boston. H. 12 in.

51A. *Candlestick, one of a set of four.*
Boulton and Fothergill, Birmingham
1774. Birmingham Assay Office.
H. 11¾ in.

51B. *Candlestick, one of a set of four.*
Boulton and Fothergill, Birmingham
1779. Birmingham Assay Office.
H. 12 in.

52. *Cup and cover. Boulton and Fothergill, Birmingham 1777.
Birmingham Assay Office. H. 12 in.*

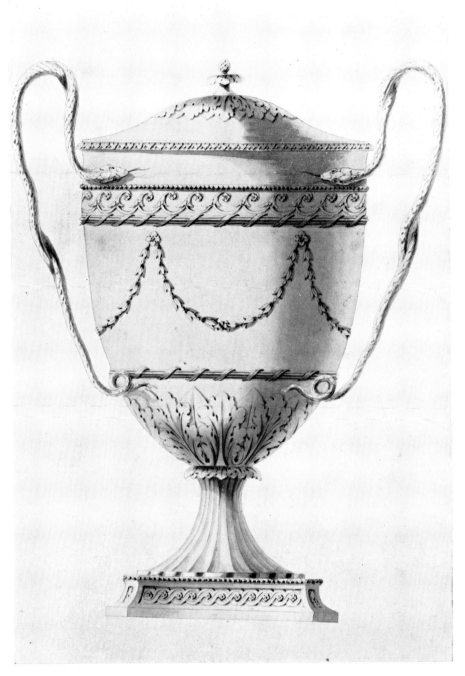

53. *Boulton and Fothergill: Pattern for a cup.*
Birmingham Reference Library.

54. *Dish ring. Boulton and Fothergill, Birmingham 1774.*
Birmingham Assay Office. H. 4½ in.

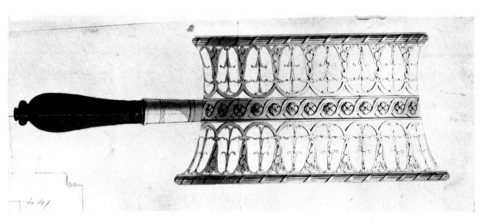

55A. *d'Hancarville: William Hamilton's Collection, 1766–7.*
Vol. II, Plate 106.
British Museum.
55B. *Boulton and Fothergill: Pattern for a dish ring.*
Birmingham Reference Library.

56A. *Sauce tureen, one of a pair. Boulton and Fothergill, Birmingham 1776.*
Birmingham Assay Office. L. 10½ in.
56B. *Sauce tureen, one of a pair. Boulton and Fothergill, Birmingham 1773.*
Birmingham Assay Office. L. 9⅛ in.

57. *Boulton and Fothergill: Patterns for sauce tureens.*
Birmingham Reference Library.

58. *Candlestick. George Ashforth & Co., Sheffield* 1774.
Victoria and Albert Museum. H. 11½ *in.*

59. *Candlestick. Maker's mark I.C., Sheffield* 1776.
Victoria and Albert Museum. H. 12¼ *in.*

60. *Candlestick. John Winter & Co., Sheffield 1774.*
City Museum, Sheffield. H. 13 in.

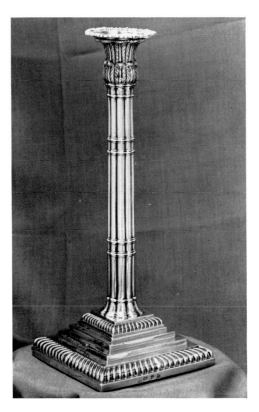

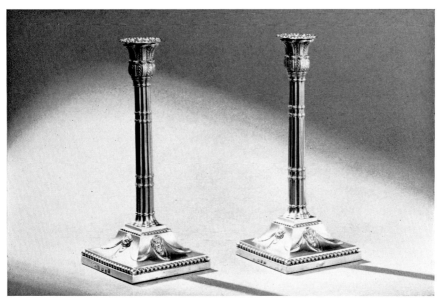

61A. *Candlestick. Maker's mark I.C., 1775.*
City Art Gallery, Manchester. H. 12¼ in.
61B. *Pair of Tapersticks, gilt. Maker's mark I.C., 1772. Messrs. Lumley.*

62. *Candlestick, Sheffield Plate. Matthew Fenton & Co., about* 1780.
City Museum, Sheffield. H. $11\frac{1}{2}$ *in.*

63. Candlestick. Samuel Roberts & Co., Sheffield 1789.
City Museum, Sheffield. H. 11½ in.

64. *Soup tureen. Thomas Heming, 1780.*
Messrs. Lumley.

65. *Soup tureen. John Wakelin and Robert Garrard,* 1792.
George Howard, Esq. H. 11½ *in.*

66. *Pair of baskets and stands, gilt. John Wakelin and William Taylor,*
baskets 1780, stands about 1785.
Messrs. Lumley.

67. *Soup tureen. John Wakelin and William Taylor, 1783.*
City of Liverpool Museums. H. 14 in.

68. *The Doncaster Race Cup, gilt. John Wakelin and William Taylor, 1786. Museum and Art Gallery, Birmingham. H. 18⅞ in.*

69A. *The Doncaster Race Cup (detail).*
69B. *Soup tureen. Andrew Fogelberg and Stephen Gilbert, 1790.*
Museum and Art Gallery, Birmingham. L. 17⅛ in.

70. *Candelabrum, one of a pair. Nicholas Dumée, 1776.*
Christie's. H. 20 in.

71A. *Candelabrum,*
one of a pair.
John Carter, 1770.
Trinity Hall,
Cambridge.
H. $17\frac{3}{4}$ *in.*

71B. *Candelabrum,*
one of a pair.
John Heming, 1771,
branches by Benjamin
Laver, 1787.
Christie's. H. 19 in.

72. *Soup tureen, one of a pair. Andrew Fogelberg, 1770. Sotheby's. L. 22¼ in.*

73. *Teapot and stand, gilt. Andrew Fogelberg and Stephen Gilbert, 1784.
Victoria and Albert Museum. H. 5¾ in.*

74. *Teapot, gilt. Andrew Fogelberg and Stephen Gilbert, 1781. Victoria and Albert Museum. H. $4\frac{1}{2}$ in.*

75A. *Sugar basin, gilt. Andrew Fogelberg, 1777.*
Victoria and Albert Museum. H. 3⅝ in.
75B. *Sauce tureen. Andrew Fogelberg and Stephen Gilbert, 1787.*
National Museum of Wales. L. 9¾ in.

76A. *Cream jug. Andrew Fogelberg and Stephen Gilbert, 1780.*
Victoria and Albert Museum. H. 5⅜ in.
76B. *Teapot. Andrew Fogelberg, 1778.*
Victoria and Albert Museum. H. 5 in.

77. *Sauce tureen. Maker's mark H.C., 1788.*
Victoria and Albert Museum. L. 7½ in.

78. *Toilet service, gilt. Daniel Smith and Robert Sharp, 1779.*
Kungl Livrustkammaren, Stockholm.

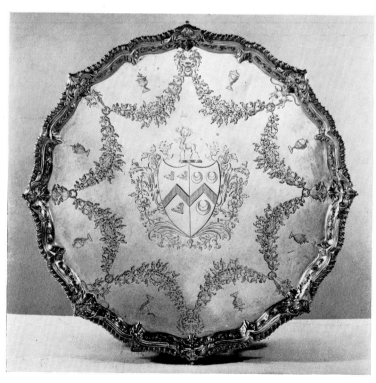

79A. *Salver. 1779. Christie's. Diam.* $24\frac{1}{2}$ *in.*
79B. *Salver. 1770. Christie's. Diam.* $16\frac{1}{2}$ *in.*

80. *Tea-urn. John Schofield, 1786.*
Courtesy, Museum of Fine Arts, Boston. H. 19 in.

81. *Tea-urn. Hester Bateman, 1790.*
Courtesy, Museum of Fine Arts, Boston. H. 24⅜ in.

82. *Teapot and stand. Hester Bateman, 1782. City Art Gallery, Bristol. H. 7 in.*

83. *Teapot. Charles Aldridge and Henry Green, 1778. Mr. and Mrs. R. P. Kellett.*
H. 4½ in.

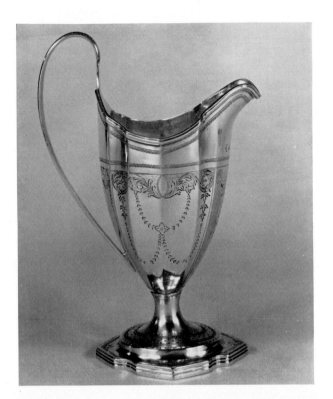

84A. *Cream jug. Maker's mark S.H., 1790.*
Victoria and Albert Museum. H. 6¾ in.
84B. *Tea-caddy. Henry Chawner, 1786.*
Mr. and Mrs. R. P. Kellett. H. 5¾ in.

85. *Jug. J. Denzilow, 1781.*
Sir William Brooksbank Bt. H. 12 in.

86. *Jug. Charles Wright, 1778.*
Royal Scottish Museum. H. 13½ *in.*

87A. *Bougie box. Joseph Heriot, 1790. Dr. Kay Sharp. H. 3⅜ in.*
87B. *Argyle. Henry Chawner, 1786. Private collection,
on loan to the City Art Gallery, Bristol. H. 9 in.*

88. *Coffee-urn. Robert Hennell, 1788. Messrs. Bell. H.* 14 *in.*

89. *Jug. Thomas Daniel, 1790. Mr. and Mrs. R. P. Kellett. H. 13 in.*

90. *Cruet-frame. Hester Bateman, 1788.*
Victoria and Albert Museum. H. 9 in.

91A. *d'Hancarville: William Hamilton's Collection,*
1766–7. Vol. III, Plate 68.
British Museum.
91B. *Cruet-frame, gilt. John Schofield, 1793.*
Earl of Lonsdale. L. 20¾ *in.*

92. *Cruet-frame, gilt. John Schofield, 1789. Victoria and Albert Museum. L. 21 in.*

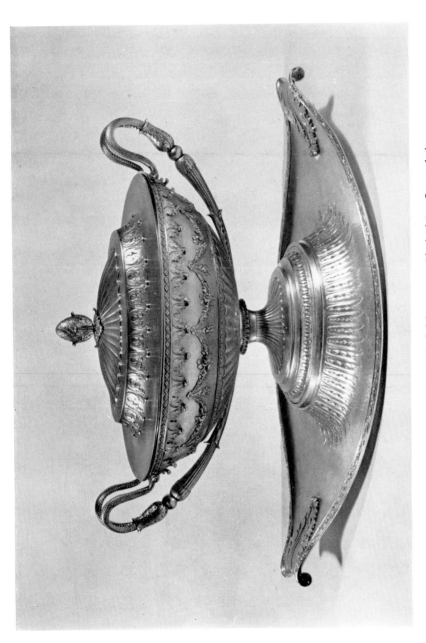

93. Soup tureen. John Schofield, 1791. Christie's. L. 23¼ in.

94. *Candelabrum, one of a pair. John Schofield,* 1781.
Mrs. Hiatt-Baker. H. 20 *in.*

95A. *Candelabrum, one of a pair. John Schofield, 1794.*
Temple Newsam House, Leeds. H. 18½ in.
95B. *Pair of chamber candlesticks. John Schofield, 1791.*
Victoria and Albert Museum. H. 3¾ in.

96. *Candlestick, gilt, one of a set of four. John Schofield, 1791–2.*
Earl of Lonsdale. H. 13¾ in.